Contents

Preface

Acknowledgments

I feel compelled to quickly thank the people who helped out in one way or another with the creation of this book. The MooTools development team deserves thanks for writing the library—Valerio Proietti in particular for starting and running the whole project and for helping out with the technical editing of this book. Ditto for Harald Kirschner, who also helped out with the technical editing.

I'd like to thank CNET, who basically paid me to learn all this stuff and contribute to MooTools. I'd like to give mad props to the fine people at Apress, especially my copy editor, Ami. Previously I would have always said, "Whoever does QA for code I write are my favorite people because they find my mistakes and make me look better." I'm going to have to add copy editors to that list as they make me seem like a far more learned man.

Finally I'd like to thank my patient, supportive, and humble wife who insisted that I dedicate this book to her, which, of course, I do.

A Note on the Code Formatting in This Book

I'd like to take a moment to note that throughout the code examples in this book, you'll see some occassionally odd code layouts. The margins of the book allow for only 56 characters per line before it wraps, and this presented a lot of challenges. My intention in the layouts in these situations was to format the code in a way that was most legible, not in a way that illustrated how I actually format the code I write. I mention it here lest you emulate the bizarre indentations you may encounter here.

Introduction

Over the past several years, JavaScript has undergone some serious changes while simultaneously becoming more and more important to both developers and users of the Web. By now, people just expect pages to be interactive, and it's up to you, the web developer, to meet those expectations and, when possible, exceed them.

Say you went to a web site today and encountered an item—a video, a story, a photo, a download—and next to that item's title was a five-star rating system with an invitation for you to click a star to rate it. Without thinking about it, you'd expect to be able to click the star of your choice and see the rating change. It might not surprise you if the page reloaded to ask you to register or log in, but the next time you rated something, you'd expect the rating to change to match your choice. But if every time you clicked a star the whole page reloaded, you'd feel something was wrong. Maybe you wouldn't be able to put your finger on it (most users certainly wouldn't think JavaScript or Ajax might be behind the problem), but something would feel odd.

The users who visit your site will have expectations that the site behave like the others they go to, and if yours doesn't, even if it looks great and has awesome content, it'll feel old. This might not drive people from using your site, but it will certainly result in less usage of the features you develop.

To meet these expectations, you'll find that you can't do it with the skill scts traditionally required to build a web site. Back-end developers of Java, Perl, PHP, Python, Ruby, and so forth often find writing JavaScript to be tedious and fraught with frustration when dealing with the browser quirks, while the people who spend most of their time working on the client side— creating the design, HTML, CSS, and images—often don't have a lot of serious programming experience.

Because the functionality that users increasingly expect is robust, developers who actually know how to program find themselves working on the client side. This means graphic designers must work closely with engineers, who typically don't think about interaction and interfaces.

JavaScript Frameworks

User expectations have driven application development, resulting in Ajax, animation, drag and drop, and other UI concepts making their way into the web browsing experience. Until a few years ago, accomplishing any of these things in JavaScript was painful and unpleasant, and consequently avoided. That all changed, though, with the introduction of *JavaScript frameworks*.

The idea behind a JavaScript framework is that it will abstract all the code you write from the engine that executes it. This helps developers overcome the most frustrating part of working with JavaScript: the environment—the browser—is one over which you as a developer have no control. Without getting into the history of JavaScript and the various competing standards that were implemented in each new generation of browsers, it is sufficient to say that browsers don't all behave the same way, which can also be said of how they handle HTML and CSS.

Why You Should Use a JavaScript Framework

JavaScript frameworks help alleviate the problems I just mentioned and bring a whole host of other benefits to the environment. Most notably, JavaScript frameworks

- Abstract your code from the runtime environment (the browser) so that various environment quirks can be handled by the framework and new quirks that are introduced subsequently can be managed in one place.

- Create a foundation base of code on which you can build and grow.

- Create a common environment for groups to contribute (with their own extensions, plug-ins, and bug fixes).

- Encourage the use of similar patterns across disparate web sites so that users can reuse the knowledge they learn (clicking five stars to rate something, for example).

Of all the frameworks that hit the market in the last few years, Prototype.js (`http://www.prototypejs.org`) was perhaps the most influential. Released in 2005, it remains one of the most well-written and robust frameworks, and it gained a great deal of acceptance and praise from developers who were on the edge of client-side development.

Prototype.js did three things that made it an instant hit:

- It introduced concepts and shortcuts that became instant standards for JavaScript development, making things like Ajax and DOM selection easy to do.

- It extended native objects like `Strings`, `Arrays`, and `Functions` (but not `Elements`) to add functionality that wasn't built into JavaScript already.

- It showed people that this kind of thing was even possible.

Of all the contributions that Prototype.js offered (and continues to offer; it's still very much supported and in development), it's that last item that was, from my perspective, the most important gift. It showed developers that writing a framework that made JavaScript itself better and easier and even kind of fun was possible.

About MooTools

This book is about *MooTools*, a JavaScript framework, primarily authored by Valerio Proietti, that gets some of its original inspiration from Prototype.js as well as from other sources (most notably Dean Edwards' *Base* library). Originally, MooTools began when Valerio released an add-on to Prototype.js called Moo.fx (which is still available at `http://moofx.mad4milk.net`) in October 2005. It was a lightweight

(3KB!) effects library that was quite popular for both its ease of use and its small size.

Not content to just release an add-on for Prototype, Valerio began work on his own framework, MooTools (which stands for My Object-Oriented Tools), and released it in September 2006. The reason he started this task was because Prototype.js, which added numerous shortcuts to the prototypes of `Array`, `String`, `Function`, and so on, didn't extend the `Element` prototype, and he was tired of repeatedly typing the prototype's `Element` generic.

At its heart, MooTools is a JavaScript framework that provides those three essential things that I mention earlier about Prototype.js: it provides shortcuts and foundation classes that make doing common things easy, it extends native objects to add functionality to them, and, perhaps most importantly, the library itself serves as an illustration of how to write JavaScript well, and, more specifically, how to write JavaScript using MooTools.

These concepts aren't necessarily unique to MooTools; indeed, nearly all JavaScript frameworks (and there are a LOT of them) do these things to varying degrees of success. What does make MooTools unique is its coding style, its well-rounded offering, and its basic philosophical approach to its continued development. The defining characteristics of MooTools are as follows:

- Don't duplicate code.
- Add functionality that fits in principle with JavaScript's own design philosophy.
- If there's a good standard in place that works well but is not yet implemented, implement the standard.
- Extend native objects (`String`, `Function`, `Array`, `Element`, `Event`, and `Number`) as JavaScript was designed to do.

- Write clean, clear, well-named code that is understandable when read by anyone with the skills to understand it.

- Be careful not to demand too much of the browser (memory, CPU cycles, etc.).

- Abstract as much away from the browser as possible.

- Whenever possible, make it still feel like you're writing JavaScript.

- Make it easy. Make it fun. Make it inspiring.

- Make it modular.

MooTools vs. Other Frameworks

When people ask me which framework to choose, I can only give them my opinion, which is that you really can't go wrong with Dojo, Yahoo! User Interface (YUI), Prototype, jQuery, or MooTools (there are others out there, so this short list is by no means definitive). These frameworks are all good choices. They all have their different focuses and approaches to problems. Some have very different philosophies and styles, but ultimately they are well written, efficient, and well supported.

MooTools and Prototype both believe strongly in altering the prototypes of native elements (String, Array, Function, etc.—except Object, never Object!) as well as offering numerous methods on these prototypes to help you work with them. YUI, jQuery, and Dojo don't do this. Both YUI and jQuery are highly namespaced, which makes them ideal for environments you don't control completely (e.g., where there might be third-party JavaScript, such as ads), while MooTools and Prototype won't play nice with other frameworks or environments that use function names like $() or modify the native objects themselves. The only downsides to the namespacing: in the case of YUI, the code is sometimes a little verbose, and frameworks that maintain all their methods in a namespace will always be slightly slower than methods added to native prototypes, although it's unlikely that this speed hit will be noticeable to you unless you are iterating over a *lot* of objects. These things are not bad things—it's just the way these frameworks are.

The advantage to modifying the native elements (aside from a slight speed advantage) is that you can add methods to these elements and extend their functionality. It's the difference between `"hi".alert()` and `alert("hi")`. It's subtle, but the former example is how JavaScript itself works. The downside is that if you define a method (like, say, `Array.each`), and something else in your environment (another script) defines the same thing, one is overwritten. The upside is a more elegant model for adding functionality to things (at least I think so).

Additionally, some frameworks focus on re-creating a somewhat traditional inheritance model. MooTools focuses on this and highly encourages code reuse and modular designs. All frameworks have methods to create reusable code—I'm not saying they don't. But this is the heart of MooTools, and not all frameworks can make that claim. JavaScript has a prototypal inheritance model (see "Prototypal Inheritance" in the Appendix), and MooTools creates a structure to take advantage of this model in a way that will be more familiar to developers used to languages like Java.

MooTools also is designed in a modular fashion so that you don't need all of it to make a page work. If you only need Ajax, you can deliver less JavaScript, and therefore fewer bytes.

If I were to sum up what makes MooTools special, it's that it makes JavaScript itself better. It focuses on the JavaScript programming language and seeks to streamline it, but not deviate from the basic principles of what makes JavaScript JavaScript. It's not trying to look like CSS, and it's not trying to look like C++ or Java (although its class architecture is certainly more similar to Java than traditional JavaScript in some ways). Other frameworks do this, too (and here I'm thinking of Prototype.js). What MooTools has that Prototype.js doesn't (the last time I looked anyway) is a set of powerful animation routines and plug-ins (like sortable lists and drag and drop). If you use Prototype.js and wish to have access to effects or drag and drop, you must include both it and another library like script.aculo.us or write this functionality yourself. Also, MooTools modular design takes up a much smaller footprint than Prototype and script.aculo.us together.

I'll reiterate that choosing any of these frameworks isn't a bad thing to do. Look at the strengths of the other options. Choose the one that suits your needs and your design principles and offers the right mix of flexibility and functionality.

About the Author

I'm a product manager by trade, but I started my career as an interface designer in the early days of the Web. I've worked at numerous startups, including my current one, Iminta (http://www.iminta.com). In 2004, CNET hired me as a product manager for the development and launch of Download.com Music. In late 2005, I started focusing on JavaScript for the network, as it was always an interest of mine since my days doing interface design in the mid-1990s. I began blogging on an internal blog for CNET, trying to spread the knowledge I was aggregating. In February 2006, I began publicly blogging on the topic at my blog, Clientside (http://clientside.cnet.com/).

At first, most of my effort was focused on Prototype.js, but when MooTools launched its suite of code in late 2006, I quickly became a convert and devoted my energy to it.

Why did I choose MooTools? A few reasons, many of which had to do with CNET's needs and some of which had to do with my own tastes. For starters, I always admired how much power Valerio Proietti managed to cram into Moo.fx. It was a 3KB effects library so cleanly written and manicured that I marveled at its artistry. I learned a lot from that 3KB.

When MooTools launched, I quickly read through the source code and learned more.

In addition to that was the modular design of the library. Prototype.js is a relatively large library, and even with it in your environment you still needed other libraries (like Moo.fx) to really make the most of it. MooTools offered a modular design that let you choose which things you needed for any given project.

Finally, MooTools was just more well rounded for the kind of work that we at CNET were doing. CNET wasn't in the business of authoring the next webmail client to compete with Yahoo or Gmail. We had busy HTML pages that we wanted to add some interaction to, and MooTools seemed to be perfect for it.

After I made this decision, I immediately began contributing to the MooTools project. I authored all the original documentation (at that time there were no docs; but to be fair, almost none of the other frameworks had comprehensive documentation either) and then the first comprehensive tutorial—the Mootorial (`http://www.mootorial.com`), which is the foundation of this book and the reason that I was approached to author it.

Since I first started using it, MooTools has grown and matured dramatically, and it offers much of the same functionality that Prototype.js and other frameworks offer. What makes it remain my choice is the artistic elegance of the code itself and the design aesthetic that shapes its development. Simply put, MooTools makes writing JavaScript *fun*.

I do commit code, but it's a rare occurrence these days. Instead, I tend to author my own plug-ins and release those for others to use while communicating with the development team frequently and offering feedback to new features and changes. On occasion, something I write will get consumed by MooTools.

About This Book

As I mention in the preceding section, I wrote the original documentation (though it's now maintained by the developer group) and the online counterpart to this book. The online tutorial (the Mootorial) is comprehensive in that it covers all the methods and classes in MooTools, but it doesn't cover all the nuances of writing good MooTools code.

The online tutorial is meant to be a more thorough introduction than the documentation and a good place to go just to see something in action, but it's not a great place to go if JavaScript is still somewhat new to you or if some of the key concepts used by MooTools aren't familiar.

This book is meant to be more complete. If the documentation and demos available at the MooTools site (`http://mootools.net`) aren't enough to help you learn the framework, and the online Mootorial isn't clear to you, this book is the place to start. Unlike the online resources, this book aims to be a cookbook with clear illustrations and time spent on those nuances that you may not pick up on with the online materials.

Who This Book Is For

This book is not meant for people who don't know any programming. For experienced JavaScript developers, this book should be useful for quickly learning MooTools and as a good reference book to have on the shelf. Hopefully, it will also be useful if you're trying to decide whether MooTools is the right framework for you.

Experienced developers of other languages (Java, PHP, Ruby, Python, Perl, etc.) who have fooled around with JavaScript a little, but have shied away from JavaScript because of its environment (the browser), or maybe because JavaScript just didn't seem like a "real" programming language, should find this book illustrative of how powerful JavaScript, and MooTools in particular, can be.

This book is **NOT** for beginning programmers or for those with no programming experience. Readers should be familiar with object-oriented programming practices and ideally should have an understanding of JavaScript's prototypal inheritance model and functional programming practices (also known as lambda), though these topics are reviewed in this book's appendix.

What You Need to Know

Readers should be familiar with the basic syntax of JavaScript as well as the Document Object Model (DOM) presented by the browsers. Experience with HTML and CSS is also obviously necessary.

Finally, you should be familiar with basic debugging practices for DOM scripting. The excellent Firefox plug-in *Firebug* is a must-have for this kind of development, so you should have experience using it or similar applications for debugging.

If you aren't familiar with these things, I suggest you check out *Accelerated DOM Scripting with Ajax, APIs, and Libraries* by Jonathan Snook et al. (Apress, 2007). I also recommend the following online resources:

- **The MooTools Blog**: `http://blog.mootools.net`. Also be sure to check out the "Help, I don't know JavaScript" page on this site at `http://blog.mootools.net/2007/6/5/help-i-dont-know-javascript`.

- **W3Schools**: `http://www.w3schools.com`

- **YUI Theater (specifically the videos on JavaScript and Firebug)**: `http://developer.yahoo.com/yui/theater/`

- **Clientside (my blog)**: `http://clientside.cnet.com`

- **Ajaxian**: `http://www.ajaxian.com`

Summary

JavaScript has come a long way in the last few years, but so have user expectations. Writing JavaScript has become more important and now consumes an ever larger part of the resource pie, both in time spent to create a web site and the bytes delivered to the browser.

Using a good JavaScript framework will help everyone who spends time on your web site, whether they are making the site with you or visiting it. JavaScript is a highly expressive and powerful language, and when you have mastered it and can make full use of a framework like MooTools, your visitors will notice. Once you get past the basics, you can start imagining user experiences that are fun and fluid, and that's the whole point of putting in the time with something like MooTools.

Chapter 1: Getting Started with MooTools

In this chapter, I'll cover some key steps and concepts that you should understand before you start writing code with MooTools. For anyone familiar with modern DOM scripting principles, most of this chapter can be skimmed over, but if you're new to this stuff, don't miss out, as it'll save you some headaches.

Here I'll cover the following:

- Downloading MooTools
- Using MooTools' modular design
- Understanding compatibility issues for upgrading from one version to the next
- Adding MooTools to your page(s) after you've downloaded it
- Coding for reuse
- Understanding concatenation and compression

Downloading MooTools

Downloading MooTools is pretty straightforward, but you have some options to consider and some choices to make.

Open up `http://www.mootools.net` in your browser, and then click the Download tab (or just skip to `http://www.MooTools.net/download`).

You'll get a page that looks like this:

Here you can download the MooTools core compressed or uncompressed. I recommend using the uncompressed version for development and the compressed version for your live site. I'll cover some methods to compress your own copy along with the code you write later in this chapter.

Downloading MooTools Official Plug-Ins

The Core download includes all the basic portions of the MooTools library needed to author Ajax, effects, and your own classes as well as all the extentions to the native objects (`Element`, `Array`, `String`, etc.). It does not, however, include some of the additional functionality that is available from the official MooTools library. To get these add-ons, you'll need to click the More Builder link on the right of the download page. Doing so will give you an interface where you can check off the additional plugins you want and let you download them as a separate file:

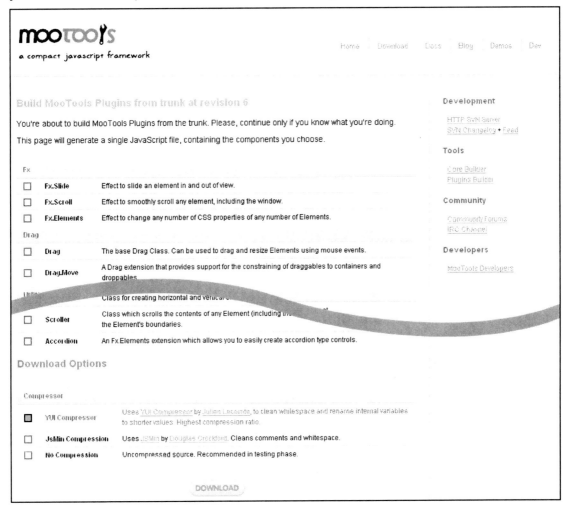

Here you can download plug-ins that let you make elements draggable, create accordion type controls or tooltips, and more. Just check off the scripts you want and then select your compression and download it.

Core Builder

You can also, if you choose, build your own custom library instead of downloading the core file from the main download page. This can be useful if you're building, say, a mobile app and you just want some of the basic functionality that MooTools has to offer. To build your own core, click the Core Builder link on the right. You'll get an interface just like the More Builder with all the files that comprise the MooTools core. If you were to select all these and download them, you would get a file that had the same contents as the file listed in the first step earlier.

Don't get overwhelmed by all the download options. I'll cover them all in the coming pages.

Making Use of MooTools' Modular Design

MooTools is designed so that you can include only the JavaScript you need for your page. Part of the MooTools code base is a dependency map that allows this download page to fill in any gaps for what you need for your application. If, for example, you need to use the `Fx.Tween` class, just click the Fx.Tween.js option, and all the dependencies for that file are automatically selected for you.

Tip   For development purposes, you might want to download the whole library. I'll stress that you shouldn't launch your application like this; it's really rare for an application to need everything MooTools has to offer.

However, if you want to get it all, it can get tedious to click everything on the list, so here's a shortcut: open Firebug and execute the following in the console to check all the items for you to download:

```
Download.all()
```

Compatibility

With each release of MooTools, there is a corresponding compatibility script that will alias function and variable names to their counterparts in the newer version. This adds more code to your environment, but not much, and if you have a lot of code written for an earlier version, this can help you transition to the newer release.

Note   When using MooTools, you should always reference only the variables and methods outlined in the documentation. Though classes have more methods and properties than are defined in the documentation, these are considered private, and the compatibility scripts that accompany each release maintain only the public methods and properties. All the others are considered private, so if you reference them in your own code, you'll have issues when you upgrade.

Compression Options

MooTools provides several options for compressing the code it delivers to you when you download it. Compressing the code doesn't change the way you use it, but rather removes all the extra spaces and transforms inner variable names to save space. The result is a much smaller file than one with all the indentation and line breaks.

The compression options you have with your download are

- **YUI Compressor**: This compressor is the most efficient and is what you should use when you're ready to release your code.

- **No Compression**: The source code is delivered unaltered.

For development, I recommend turning compression off entirely so that you can easily debug any errors you encounter. If you use a compressed version for development and get an error, the line number will always be line #1, because compression removes all the line breaks.

Adding MooTools to Your Page(s)

Now that you have the JavaScript file, you need to add it to your HTML documents. Once you've done that, you can write JavaScript using MooTools methods and classes. Here's a simple example document that illustrates how to add MooTools to your page(s):

```
<!DOCTYPE html PUBLIC "-//W3C//DTD XHTML 1.0 Strict//EN"
    "http://www.w3.org/TR/xhtml1/DTD/xhtml1-strict.dtd">
<html xmlns="http://www.w3.org/1999/xhtml" xml:lang="en"
  lang="en" dir="ltr">
  <head profile="http://gmpg.org/xfn/11">
    <meta http-equiv="Content-Type" content="text/html;
     charset=UTF-8" />
    <title>Your title</title>
    <script type="text/javascript"
      src="MooTools.js"></script>
    <script type="text/javascript"
      src="yourSiteCode.js"></script>
    <script type="text/javascript">
      //or write some code in-line
    </script>
  </head>
  <body>....</body>
</html>
```

Coding for Reuse

If you divide your code into two types—implementation code and classes that are designed for reuse—you'll find that your work can pay off for faster development, maintenance, and a smaller code base that has to be delivered to your users.

If you are going to write code to animate several images in a carousel, consider writing a generic class that does that, with variables and options passed in and set whenever the class is invoked. When you explore the section of this book on classes (see Chapter 7), you'll see how these can be extended and reused later.

What's more, using generic classes allows you to make your implementation code a much more brief set of instructions that just creates instances of these classes for individual pages. You can then deliver two JavaScript files to every page on your site: the common code that includes MooTools and the implementation code for that specific page. The fewer files you send to the browser, the faster your site will be; and with your code clearly separated, you'll find it much easier to maintain and reuse.

Compression

As mentioned earlier, you can download MooTools with compression enabled or unaltered. When developing, it's helpful to use the uncompressed code so that errors yield actual line numbers, and the code is readable.

The same holds true for the code you write. If you have a lot of JavaScript on your site, it's courteous to your visitors to compress the code you write in addition to MooTools.

I recommend the YUI Compressor (`http://developer.yahoo.com/yui/compressor/` and also `http://www.julienlecomte.net/yuicompressor/`) provided by Yahoo. It can be run at the command line or as part of a larger app. It even comes with a web interface in the distribution. All you need is Java to use it.

Using the YUI Compressor

The way that MooTools itself works is a good illustration of how to maintain and deliver JavaScript. It's much easier to maintain a set of small files that each contain a specific set of functionality, but delivering these files individually will slow down your site.

MooTools provides SVN (a.k.a. Subversion) access to download these small files, but offers a download page that lets you download a compressed version of the files you need for your application.

In my own experience, this practice also works well for your code.

In my environment, I use a set of shell scripts that will concatenate a library from the various source files that I maintain, and then process the resulting file through the YUI Compressor to output the compact file.

Here's an example of what that kind of script looks like:

```
cat "MooTools/1-11/Core/Core.js" > global.js
cat "MooTools/1-11/Class/Class.js" >> global.js
cat "MooTools/1-11/Class/Class.Extras.js" >> global.js
cat "mycode/slideshow.js" >> global.js
cat "mycode/carousel.js" >> global.js
java -jar yuicompressor-2.2.4.jar -o
   global.compressed.js global.js
```

The result is a set of two files: global.js, which is uncompressed, and global.compressed.js, which is much smaller. I can use the former for development and debugging and the latter for delivery to the visitors of my site.

When editing the files that I maintain, I can just save my changes, run the shell script, and refresh my browser.

There are more sophisticated methods for doing this sort of thing with Ant targets and the like, but if you know how to author those, this simple example should be enough to illustrate the concept.

Chapter 2: Reviewing MooTools

This book is divided into chapters that correspond with the functionality found in the MooTools library so that you can easily use it as a reference, by paging through to find the information you're seeking. In this way, it is very much like the online counterpart to this book (`http://www.mootorial.com`).

Each chapter will cover a basic set of functionality (like effects, for example) and feature the following:

- A short overview of the syntax of the methods and classes
- Code examples illustrating how to use the classes, methods, and functions
- A review of the important functionality provided and any nuances that will help you use the it properly

In this manner, each chapter will attempt to illustrate not only *how* to use MooTools, but also *why* it works the way it does.

Note   In all cases, it's always a good idea to look at the MooTools source code to gain a deeper understanding of how it works. There is no better illustration of how to use MooTools than MooTools itself. Using the library as a template for your own code will not only help you understand it better, but also help you write your code in a Moo way.

MooTools File Structure

MooTools is broken up into numerous files to make it easy to download only the part that you need for your page to work (see "Making Use of MooTools' Modular Design" in the Introduction). Part of the process of organizing the code into the various libraries to make this modular design possible requires that some functionality be split up. For example,

`Core/Core.js` is required for all of MooTools, and it includes numerous shortcut methods as well as the base functionality for the `Hash` native object. But `Hash` has its own script in `Native/Hash.js`, which contains much more functionality. The functionality in `Core.js` is there just to support other scripts that need it.

This splitting up of functionality isn't reflected in the organization of this book; in order to illustrate how to use the library, it's best that I keep ideas that are similar next to each other.

In each section that I illustrate a method, function, or class, I'll also note its location in the library whenever it isn't obvious so you can find it in the code.

Manifest of MooTools Scripts

Here is a list of every file in the MooTools library, along with what it does and when you'll use it.

MooTools is broken into two separate libraries: The "Core" and plug-ins, which MooTools has in a repository called "More."

The MooTools Core

When you visit MooTools and download the main library (the Core), you'll get all the following files.

Core/Core.js

What it does: Defines the `Native` class and numerous helper functions used throughout MooTools. `Core.js` also defines the base functionality for the `Hash` and `Array` native objects.

When you'll use it: MooTools uses all the methods in this script. You yourself will use several of them, though likely not the `Native` function, as MooTools instantiates instances of the `Native` class for nearly all the native objects (specifically, MooTools creates them for `Array`, `Element`, `Event`, `Function`, `Hash`, `Number`, and `Function`).

Core/Browser.js

What it does: Defines the `Browser` hash and identifies various properties about the client running library (i.e., the user's browser). `Browser.js` also defines the `Window` and `Document` native objects.

When you'll use it: MooTools itself uses the methods of this script for scripts that help fix browser quirks. You'll need to reference the properties and methods defined in this script whenever you have your own code that has conditionals based on the client (e.g., if you have code that should work differently for IE than it does in Safari or Firefox).

Class/Class.js

What it does: Defines `Class` and its methods and properties.

When you'll use it: `Class` is a powerful method for creating reusable functionality. This method is at the heart of MooTools, so you'll use it all the time whether you're authoring a class or instantiating one.

Class/Class.Extras.js

What it does: Defines the `Events`, `Chain`, and `Options` classes.

When you'll use it: The three classes defined in this script can be implemented into others, providing common, reusable patterns employed throughout MooTools and useful in your own work.

Element/Element.js

What it does: Extends the `Element` native object, providing numerous shortcut, selection, and initialization methods.

When you'll use it: Like all the scripts in the Native directory, Element.js extends the native DOM Element. This is one of the most important scripts in the library. The Element files are located in their own directory (instead of in the Native directory with the other scripts) because Element.*.js requires all the other Native scripts.

Element/Element.Dimensions.js

What it does: Extends the Element native with methods to inspect the location and dimensions of that element.

When you'll use it: Whenever you need to work with size, scrolling, or positioning of elements and the document.

Element/Event.js

What it does: Extends the native Event object with element-specific methods, defines the functionality to create custom events, and includes the mouseenter, mouseleave, and mousewheel custom events.

When you'll use it: Whenever you attach an event listener to a DOM element (click, load, mouseover, etc.), the method you attach is, by default, passed the event that fired it. Element.Events.js extends elements to make attaching events and managing the Event object easier.

Element/Style.js

What it does: Defines methods used to alter the style properties of elements.

When you'll use it: Whenever you wish to alter the style of a DOM element, you'll use the methods defined in Element.Style.js.

Fx/Fx.js

What it does: Defines the base functionality for all the Fx.*.js scripts.

When you'll use it: You probably won't use `Fx.js` directly. It's only useful if you wish to write your own effect extension.

Fx/Fx.CSS.js

What it does: Defines the animation logic for transitioning style properties.

When you'll use it: It's used indirectly through `Fx.Tween`, `Fx.Morph`, and `Fx.Elements`, but, like `Fx`, it's unlikely that you'll use it directly unless you extend it to write your own effect.

Fx/Fx.Morph.js

What it does: Defines the `Fx.Morph` effect.

When you'll use it: `Fx.Morph` is used to transition more than one CSS property at once (e.g., height *and* width).

Fx/Fx.Transitions.js

What it does: Defines numerous transitions that can be used by any effect.

When you'll use it: `Fx` (and therefore the classes that extend it) comes with a basic linear transition, but `Fx.Transitions.js` defines a dozen more including `bounce`, `circ`, `expo`, `elastic`, and others. Additionally, `Fx.Transitions.js` defines methods that you can use to write your own.

Fx/Fx.Tween.js

What it does: Defines the `Fx.Tween` effect.

When you'll use it: `Fx.Tween` is used to transition a single CSS property (height, width, color, etc.).

Native/Array.js

What it does: Extends the `Array` native with additional methods.

When you'll use it: Whenever you work with data in array format, you'll benefit from the 20 or so methods added to its prototype by `Array.js`.

Native/Event.js

What it does: Extends the native `Event` object to grant it cross-browser stability.

When you'll use it: `Event.js` works well with `Element.Event.js`. The former focuses on extending the `Event` native with properties and methods to remove the inconsistencies found in different browser implementations of the `Event` object, while the latter implements methods and properties on the `Element` native to make it easy to attach event listeners and manage them.

Native/Function.js

What it does: Extends the native `Function` object with numerous methods that enhance functional programming.

When you'll use it: You'll use the methods added by MooTools to the native `Function` object constantly. Functional programming (see "Functional Programming (a.k.a. Lambda)" in the Appendix) requires that you interact with `Function` objects constantly, and `Function.js` includes several methods that make that management easier.

Native/Hash.js

What it does: Extends the native `Object` when you initialize it (`new Hash()`).

When you'll use it: Because all native objects in JavaScript inherit from `Object`, modifying its prototype is universally considered bad form. MooTools therefore provides an enhanced `Object` with various properties and methods applied to it, just like it does for the other natives (`Array`, `Function`, etc.). However, unlike the other native scripts, this script requires you to initialize any object that you wish to apply these methods to.

Native/Number.js

What it does: Extends the native Number object to add numerous helpful methods.

When you'll use it: Whenever you're doing math or managing numbers or even just iterating a function a specified number of times, the methods in Number.js will help make the process simpler.

Native/String.js

What it does: Extends the native String object to add numerous helpful methods.

When you'll use it: Like Number.js, String.js makes inspecting and altering strings much easier.

Request/Request.js

What it does: Defines the Request class, an XMLHttpRequest wrapper.

When you'll use it: This is MooTools' Ajax class. It provides a rich interface to the native XMLHttpRequest, or XHR.

Request/Request.HTML.js

What it does: Extends the Request class to add functionality specific to updating content in the DOM with HTML retrieved from the server.

When you'll use it: Whenever your Ajax request retrieves HTML that is used to update the contents of a DOM element (a common practice).

Request/Request.JSON.js

What it does: Extends the `Request` class to automatically manage the receiving of JSON data.

When you'll use it: Whenever you are receiving data in a JSON notation (the result of converting a native JavaScript `Object` to a `String`).

Selectors/Selectors.js

What it does: Adds advanced CSS querying capabilities for selecting elements.

When you'll use it: `Element.js` includes the `$$` function to collect objects out of the DOM as well as element methods such as `Element.getElements`. These methods by default only accept tag names for filters (`$$('div')` gets all the divs on a page). When you include `Selectors.js`, you can use any CSS expression with these methods to select elements from the DOM.

Utilities/Cookie.js

What it does: Defines a set of methods in the `Cookie` namespace for managing cookie values.

When you'll use it: Whenever you want to read, write, or remove cookies.

Utilities/DomReady.js

What it does: Defines the `domready` custom event.

When you'll use it: The `domready` event is used to delay the execution of your page initialization code until after all the HTML has been delivered to the browser and is available in memory. It's crucial that you don't interact with the DOM until after it's loaded using this custom event. The `onload` event on the window can be used the same way, but has the negative quality of waiting for every image to load before running.

Utilities/JSON.js

What it does: Contains methods for managing data in JSON format.

When you'll use it: Whenever you need to encode or decode JSON.

Utilities/Swiff.js

What it does: Serves as a wrapper for embedding SWF movies. Supports (and fixes) external interface communication.

When you'll use it: Whenever you wish to embed SWF (Flash) objects.

The MooTools Plug-Ins: "More"

When you download the plug-ins for MooTools, you can choose any of the following files to include. These are the "official" MooTools plug-ins, though numerous third-party plug-ins are also available (which I cover in Chapter 12).

Fx/Fx.Elements.js

What it does: Defines the `Fx.Elements` effect.

When you'll use it: When you need to alter CSS properties on several elements at once, it's more efficient to use a single instance of `Fx.Elements` than to have several instances of `Fx.Tween` or `Fx.Morph`.

Fx/Fx.Scroll.js

What it does: Defines the `Fx.Scroll` effect.

When you'll use it: `Fx.Scroll` is used to smoothly scroll any DOM element, including the window.

Fx/Fx.Slide.js

What it does: Defines the Fx.Slide effect.

When you'll use it: The Fx.Slide effect moves an element in and out of view kind of like window blinds. A container element crops out the view of the element as it slides in or out.

Drag/Drag.js

What it does: Defines the base functionality for dragging items in the browser window.

When you'll use it: Any time you want to have an element on your page that the user interacts with by dragging, you'll use Drag.js. You can attach any functionality to the dragging action, from resizing, to moving, to, say, changing the color of something.

Drag/Drag.Move.js

What it does: Provides support for the constraining of draggables to containers and droppables.

When you'll use it: If part of the drag functionality that you use requires the ability to drop things into containers and you wish to constrain the behavior to an area, Drag.Move.js provides basic methods to do this.

Utilities/Assets.js

What it does: Provides methods to dynamically load JavaScript, CSS, and image files into the document.

When you'll use it: If you're injecting a lot of assets into the DOM, Assets.js provides some easy methods to make the process a little easier.

Utilities /Color.js

What it does: Defines the `Color` class for creating and manipulating colors in JavaScript. It supports conversions from HSB to RGB and vice versa.

When you'll use it: If you're doing color calculations, the `Color` class contains numerous methods that are helpful.

Utilities/Group.js

What it does: Defines the `Group` class used to monitor a collection of events.

When you'll use it: Whenever you have numerous classes or elements that you wish to monitor as a collection. For instance, you would use this class if you want to execute a function only after each div on the page has been clicked.

Utilities/Hash.Cookie.js

What it does: Defines the `Hash.Cookie` class.

When you'll use it: If you have a map of keys/values that you need to store in a cookie, `Hash.Cookie` automates the process by creating or retrieving the cookie and then providing methods to get and set the values, automatically updating the cookie in the process.

Interface/Accordion.js

What it does: Defines the `Accordion` UI class.

When you'll use it: If you have a long definition list (like an FAQ) or a menu that needs to expand, the `Accordion` class provides a nice way to make that interactive.

Interface/Scroller.js

What it does: Defines the `Scroller` class, which scrolls the contents of any element (including the `window`) when the mouse reaches the element's boundaries.

When you'll use it: If you have draggable elements on the page, and they should be draggable to a location that is scrolled either off screen (in the case of the `window`) or out of view (in the case of an overflowed DOM element), you need some method for users to drag things from their location to their off-screen targets. The `Scroller` class provides the functionality to automatically scroll the DOM element or the `window` when users drag an element near the boundaries of the area that needs to scroll.

Interface/Slider.js

What it does: Defines the `Slider` class with two elements: a knob and a container.

When you'll use it: This basic UI component is useful when you want users to select a value from a set of values—like how big the thumbnails on a page should be or the maximum price they are willing to pay for something.

Interface/SmoothScroll.js

What it does: Defines the `SmoothScroll` class.

When you'll use it: `SmoothScroll` automatically converts any name anchors on the page (links that reference a different location on the same page with the # value) to animate the window so it scrolls smoothly to the target location instead of just jumping there.

Interface/Sortables.js

What it does: Defines the Sortables class.

When you'll use it: Sortables lets you easily convert a collection of elements into a draggable, sortable list. You can have more than one list so that users can drag items from one list to another, dropping the item into a new location in the new list.

Interface/Tips.js

What it does: Defines the Tips class.

When you'll use it: The Tips class makes it easy to display tooltips when users hover their mouse over a given DOM element.

Chapter 3: Shortcuts and Helpful Functions

MooTools has numerous stand-alone functions that make tasks easier and take fewer keystrokes. Most of these functions are used by MooTools itself and are located in `Core/Core.js`, which is required by all of MooTools. Others are more specific to specific kinds of tasks, and you'll only have them available if you include the scripts that are needed to accomplish those tasks.

Determining the Type of an Object: *$type*

JavaScript is a loosely typed language, which allows for a great deal of expressiveness, but also results in a lot of headaches. On top of this, JavaScript does a lot of type coercion (see "Type Coercion—'Falsy' and 'Truthy' Values" in the Appendix).

Thankfully, MooTools fixes this for us developers with the `$type` function.

$type :: Core/Core.js

What it does: `$type` returns the type of the object that is passed in.

Usage:

```
$type(object) //"string", "object", or "array", etc.
```

Example:

```
var ninja = {
  wealth: 0,
  getPaid: function(howMuch){
    if ($type(howMuch) == "string") {
      ninja.wealth += parseInt(howMuch);
    } else if ($type(howMuch) == "number") {
      ninja.wealth += howMuch;
    }
  }
};
```

When you'll use it: Often, you'll be unsure whether your method is being passed a string or a number, a DOM element or its ID, and so on. $type returns the type of an object as a string ('function', 'string', etc.) or false if the object is not defined. Here are the values it returns (all strings unless noted):

- "element" if the object is a DOM element node
- "textnode" if the object is a DOM text node
- "whitespace" if the object is a DOM whitespace node
- "arguments" if the object is an arguments object
- "object" if the object is an object
- "array" if the object is an array
- "string" if the object is a string
- "number" if the object is a number
- "boolean" if the object is a Boolean
- "function" if the object is a function
- "regexp" if the object is a regular expression
- "class" if the object is a MooTools class

- "collection" if the object is a native HTML elements collection, such as `childNodes`, `getElementsByTagName`, and so on
- "window" if the object is the `window` object
- "document" if the object is the `document` object
- "date" if the object is a date
- `false` (Boolean) if the object is not defined or is none of the above

Checking Whether Values Are Defined: $defined, $chk, and $pick

Often in your code, you'll need to determine whether a variable has been defined by the user. MooTools gives you some helpful methods to simplify this basic task.

$defined :: Core/Core.js

What it does: `$defined` checks to see whether a variable is defined (i.e., not `null` or `undefined`).

Usage:

```
$defined(object)
```

Example:

```
function myFunction(arg){
  if($defined(arg)) alert('The object is defined.');
  else alert('The object is null or undefined.');
}
```

When you'll use it: This is just a shortcut for

```
value == undefined
```

Because JavaScript performs type coercion (see "Type Coercion—'Falsy' and 'Truthy' Values" in the Appendix), you can't just evaluate a value to see if it has a value. All the following examples perform type coercion:

```
if ("") ... //false
if (0) ... //false
if (null) ... //false
function test(value){
  return !!value;
};
test(); //No value passed, so it is undefined,
        //and test() returns false
```

As these examples demonstrate, $chk is a shortcut to determine whether a value has been set at all.

$chk :: Core/Core.js

What it does: $chk checks to see whether a value is defined or is zero.

Usage:

```
$chk(value)
```

Example:

```
var ninja = {
  wealth: 0,
  getPaid: function(howMuch){
    if ($chk(howMuch)) wealth += howMuch;
  }
};
```

When you'll use it: Much like $defined, $chk helps you manage type coercion. $chk will still return false for null, undefined, false, and empty strings, but it *won't* return false for zero.

$pick :: Core/Core.js

What it does: $pick returns the first defined argument passed in or null. You can pass as many arguments to $pick as you like, and the first one that is not null or undefined will be returned.

Usage:

```
$pick(var1, var2, var3, etc.)
```

Example:

```
var ninja = {
  chooseSide: function(isGood){
    ninja.isGood = $pick(isGood, ninja.side, false);
  }
};
```

In this example, when the method `chooseSide` is executed, the side of the `ninja` is set to be the value passed in. If no value is passed in, the side is set to the current state. If there is no current state, the side defaults to `ninja.isGood = false`.

When you'll use it: `$pick` is yet another shortcut. You can express its basic concept as a simple conditional:

```
function test(var1, var2){
  if(var1 == undefined) return var2;
  else return var1;
};
```

Because `$pick` lets you pass in numerous arguments, it allows for numerous of these conditionals. In the preceding `ninja` example, I use `$pick` for three values. If I were to express this as a set of `if/else` conditionals, it would look like this:

```
var ninja = {
  chooseSide: function(isGood){
    if ($defined(isGood)) {
      ninja.isGood = isGood;
    } else if (!$defined(ninja.side)) {
      ninja.isGood = false;
    }
  }
};
```

The more things you need to consider, the more conditionals you have to add. $pick is shorthand for all that logic.

Tip   You can also use the logical "or" (||) for most of these operations. For example

```
var ninja = {
  setName: function(name){
    ninja.name = name || ninja.name ||'fred';
  }
};
```

Here we store `name` as the value passed in, or the current value of `ninja.name`, or a default (`fred`). You should use $pick whenever a valid value is "falsy" (zero, an empty string, the Boolean `false`, etc.).

Working with Objects: *$extend*, *$merge*, and *$unlink*

The native object—a `Hash`-like set of key/value pairs—is something that we developers use often in modern JavaScript. Unfortunately, the language doesn't have many tools to help you manage the data in them.

JavaScript objects do not contain any native methods or properties, and while MooTools does give us a more powerful version of this (with `Hash`— see "Objects (a.k.a *Hash*)" in Chapter 4), it doesn't alter the prototype of `object` (which is an important rule in JavaScript, as all other objects— including functions and strings and arrays—inherit from the `object` prototype).

To make things easier to work with native objects, MooTools provides the following core methods.

$extend :: Core/Core.js

What it does: $extend copies all the properties from the second object passed in to the first object.

Usage:

```
$extend(object1, object2)
```

Example:

```
var firstObj = {
   'name': 'John',
   'lastName': 'Doe'
};
var secondObj = {
   'age': '20',
   'sex': 'male',
   'lastName': 'Dorian'
};
$extend(firstObj, secondObj);
//firstObj is now:
//{'name': 'John', 'lastName': 'Dorian', 'age': '20',
// 'sex': 'male'};
```

When you'll use it: The functionality defined in $extend is pretty straightforward—if you need to blend the properties of one object into another, $extend will do that for you. You should use $extend any time that you need to manage objects this way *except* when the objects being blended contain as properties other objects or arrays.

The problem is that if you use $extend on objects that *do* contain arrays or other objects as properties, you will link them together.

Here's a simple illustration in code:

```
var defaultNinja = {
    weapons: ['sword', 'star', 'stealth'],
    equipment: {
        grapple: 'iron',
        rope: '40 meters'
    }
};
var goodNinja = {
    specialAbility: 'warrior spirit',
    weakness: 'kittens'
}
$extend(goodNinja, defaultNinja);
//Now goodNinja contains the weapons array and the
//equipment object
```

In this example, both goodNinja and defaultNinja contain properties for weapons and equipment because $extend copies them from the former into the latter.

However, because they are of type array and object, respectively, they are linked—they are the same objects. If you subsequently added flying guillotine to goodNinja.weapons, both goodNinja.weapons and defaultNinja.weapons would contain that value.

This is due to the way JavaScript assigns variables to memory. Consider this code:

```
var x = 'foo';
var y = x;
x = 'bar';
//x != y;
```

Everything is fine if you're just assigning values to variables. But when you're dealing with objects, the equals sign means something a little different. If I say that two objects are equal to each other and then change a property of one of them, I change that property for both. Consider the following:

```
var myArmy = {
  ninjas: {
    side: 'evil'
  }
};
var yourArmy = {};
yourArmy.ninjas = myArmy.ninjas;
//ninjas here are the same object

yourArmy.ninjas.side = 'good';
//myArmy.ninjas.side == 'good';
//yourArmy.ninjas.side == 'good';
```

In this example, you can see that the property `ninjas` for both `myArmy` and `yourArmy` is assigned to the same object. These properties are the *same object*. Changing the value of that object using either reference changes it for both.

This is why `$extend` is only useful for objects that do not contain properties that are also objects or arrays (arrays have the same problem), and why you should use `$merge` when you have members that are themselves objects or arrays.

It's important to note that this isn't a fault with `$extend` or JavaScript; it's how JavaScript is supposed to work. Most of the time it's an asset, but occasionally when you encounter these kinds of links unintentionally, you can get some unintended results.

$merge :: Core/Core.js

What it does: `$merge` combines any number of objects recursively, dereferencing them or their subobjects from their parents.

Usage:

```
$merge(object1, object2, object3, etc.)
```

Example:

```
var obj1 = {a: 0, b: 1};
var obj2 = {c: 2, d: 3};
var obj3 = {a: 4, d: 5};
var merged = $merge(obj1, obj2, obj3);
//Returns {a: 4, b: 1, c: 2, d: 5}
//(obj1, obj2, and obj3 are unaltered)

var nestedObj1 = {a: {b: 1, c: 1}};
var nestedObj2 = {a: {b: 2}};
var nested = $merge(nestedObj1, nestedObj2);
//Returns {a: {b: 2, c: 1}}
```

When you'll use it: Any time you need to combine two objects that contain members that are objects or arrays, you should use $merge to ensure you don't link the result to the originals. $merge is slower than $extend, so you shouldn't overuse it, but care should be taken that you use $merge when you need to (see the section "*$extend* :: Core/Core.js" section earlier in this chapter on this topic).

As outlined in the discussion on $extend, $merge lets you blend objects together, but is recursive when it finds properties that are also arrays or objects. Unlike when you use $extend, you don't have to worry about linking the objects together, but you pay a performance price for this recursion.

Also, unlike $extend, $merge lets you pass it any number of objects. If any two objects contain the same properties (but different values), the last one wins.

For example:

```
ninja.garb = $merge({
  mask: 'red',
  sash: 'black'
}, {
  sash: 'white'
}); //Returns {mask: 'red', sash: 'white'}
```

When $merge encounters properties that are objects, it will execute itself on that property, blending the two properties together as illustrated in the second example in the preceding "Example" section.

Finally, unlike objects passed to $extend, objects passed to $merge are not altered. Instead, the resulting merged object is returned by the method. If you want to assign the result to one of the objects passed in, you can do that easily enough:

```
object1 = $merge(object1, object2);
```

$unlink :: Core/Core.js

What it does: $unlink will return a copy of an object or array that contains no links to the original.

Usage:

```
$unlink(array)
$unlink(object)
```

Example:

```
evilNinja.desires = ['money', 'a worthy opponent',
  'friends'];
goodNinja.desires = $unlink(evilNinja.desires);
goodNinja.desires.splice(0,1);
//goodNinja doesn't need money
```

If $unlink weren't included in this example, the desires of evilNinja would point to the same array as the desires of goodNinja, and altering one would alter the other. Including `$unlink` creates a copy of the array (or object) and breaks any of these links.

When you'll use it: MooTools bakes this method into much of its functionality, so it's not something you're likely to call upon very often. Whenever you need a copy of an array or object that contains as members other arrays or objects, you'll need to unlink them to ensure you don't pollute the original.

Iterable Helpers and Shortcuts: *$arguments, $each, $splat, $A,* and *$H*

Both arrays and objects contain members that you'll often find the need to iterate over. You can use the standard `for` loop, but this isn't a very functional way of doing things. There are some advantages to iterating over a collection and executing methods on those members (see "Functional Programming (a.k.a. Lambda)" in the Appendix).

The current specification for JavaScript includes more modern iteration methods like `Array.each` and others, but only certain browsers offer native support. MooTools extends arrays and objects (via its `Hash` class) with these methods, but it also supplies a few stand-alone iteration methods in its core that can be used on their own.

$arguments :: Core/Core.js

What it does: The `$arguments` function creates a function that returns the passed argument according to the index passed in.

Usage:

```
var argument = $argument(i);
```

Example:

```
var secondArgument = $arguments(1);
console.log(secondArgument('a','b','c')); // Alerts b
```

When you'll use it: You will likely not find yourself using it, so if you don't get why you'd want it, don't sweat it. This function is used within MooTools, which has a lot of functionality that's highly abstract. `$arguments` is an example of one of these abstract concepts that gets used in the framework itself, but it's highly unlikely that you'll find a reason in your own work to use it.

$each :: Core/Core.js

What it does: `$each` is used to iterate through iterables that are not regular arrays, such as built-in `getElementsByTagName` or `Element.childNodes` calls, arguments of a function, or objects.

Usage:

```
$each(arguments, function(value, [index or key]){
  alert(value);
}, bin
```

Example:

```
//Simple example with function referencing each value
$each([1,2,3], function(value){
  alert(value); //Alerts 1, 2, 3
});
//Same concept but the function also references
//the index of each value
$each([1,2,3], function(value, index){
  alert('the value at index ' + index + ' is ' + value);
  //Alerts
  //"the value at index 0 is 1"
  //"the value at index 1 is 2"
  //"the value at index 2 is 3"
});
//This example illustrates binding
```

```
var example = {
  say: function(msg) {
    alert(msg);
  },
  count: function(){
    $each([1,2,3], function(number) {
      this.say(number);
    }, this); //Here's the important part!
  }
};
//This example illustrates iterating over an object
$each({apple: 'red', lemon: 'yellow'},
  function (value, key) {
    alert(key + 's are ' + value);
    //Alerts
    // "apples are red"
    // "lemons are yellow"
  }, this); //The binding of 'this' is optional
```

When you'll use it: $each is an alternative way to iterate over an array or object. It's a substitute for these syntaxes:

```
//Array loop:
for(var i = 0; i < array.length; i++){ alert(array[i]) }
//Object loop:
for(key in object) { alert(object[key]) }
```

More importantly, though, is the functional nature of the method. $each accepts a function that is applied to each item in the array or object and consequently encourages the user to develop in a functional manner. It provides the benefit of the ability to bind a scope to the passed function and to make use of closures (see "'this' Binding' and "Closures" in the Appendix for more).

$splat :: Core/Core.js

What it does: $splat converts the argument passed in to an array if it is defined and not already an array.

Usage:

```
$splat(object)
```

Example:

```
$splat('hello') //['hello']
$splat([1,2,3]) //[1,2,3]
var ninja = {
  fight: function(who){
    //We don't know if who is a single enemy
    //or an array of them
    $splat(who).each(function(enemy){
      enemy.isAlive = false;
    });
  }
};
```

When you'll use it: $splat is usually written for interfaces where it's convenient to be able to hand a method a single thing or a bunch of them. If you are calling such a method and you have one thing, it's nice to just be able to call the method with that one thing. But the method itself has to deal with getting an array or a single variable. $splat will take the object passed to it and, if it's an array, just return the object; otherwise, it'll add the object to an empty array and return that.

$A :: Core/Core.js

What it does: $A creates an array from an iterable object (such as the arguments of a method or a DOM node collection). If the item passed in is an array, $A will simply return it.

Usage:

```
var myArray = $A(iterable);
```

Example:

```
var ninja = {
  weapons: [],
  equip: function(){
    $A(arguments).each(function(weapon){
      ninja.weapons.push(weapon);
    });
  }
};
ninja.equip("sword", "star", "smoke");
```

When you'll use it: $A is mostly used by MooTools for applying the Array methods to iterable objects, but it can also be useful if you want to have a function or method that takes an unspecified number of arguments by referencing $A(arguments), as in the preceding example. You could make the function require an array as its argument, but it might be easier to use if you don't. For example, see the discussion on $pick in the section "Checking Whether Values Are Defined: *$defined*, *$chk*, and *$pick*" earlier in this chapter.

$H :: Core/Core.js

What it does: $H is a shortcut to initialize an instance of Hash.

Usage:

```
$H(object)
```

Example:

```
var fooHash = $H({foo: 'bar'});
```

When you'll use it: This is just a shortcut for new Hash(obj), which returns an instance of Hash (see "Objects (a.k.a. *Hash*)" in Chapter 4 for more on Hash).

Other Shortcuts: *$clear, $empty, $lambda, $random, $time, $try*

In addition to the iteration and inspection shortcuts listed previously in this chapter, MooTools provides a few other core tricks to make using JavaScript a little more pleasant. With the exception of these stand-alone functions (and a few others in the library), almost all the other functions provided by MooTools are in methods on native objects (like `Array` or `String`) or MooTools classes (like effects).

$clear :: Core/Core.js

What it does: `$clear` clears a `timeout` or an `interval`.

Usage:

```
$clear(timer)
```

Example:

```
var timer = setTimeout(ninjas.attack, 500);
$clear(timer); //Belay that order!
```

When you'll use it: This is just a shortcut for `clearTimeout` and `clearInterval`.

$empty :: Core/Core.js

What it does: `$empty` is, surprise, an empty function. Typically, it is used as a placeholder inside event methods of classes.

Usage:

```
var callback = $empty;
```

Example:

```
var ninja = {
   afterAttack: $empty,
   attack: function(enemy) {
       enemy.isAlive = false;
       ninja.afterAttack();
   }
};
//Later
ninja.afterAttack = function(){
    ninja.weep();
};
```

When you'll use it: A common practice in MooTools is to define a
callback as an empty function (literally just `function(){}`). Then later,
the user writes some code that defines that callback as something else. In
the code that calls that callback, it doesn't have to check to see whether the
user set the function or not. If the user didn't set it, it's still just an empty
function, and there's no harm in executing it. `$empty` is just a shortcut for
`function(){}`.

$lambda :: Core/Core.js

What it does: `$lambda` creates an empty function that does nothing but
return the value passed, unless the passed-in item is a function, in which
case it calls that function.

Usage:

```
var returnTrue = $lambda(true);
```

Example:

```
myLink.addEvent('click', $lambda(false));
//Prevents a link Element from being clickable.
var test = function(item){
  return $lambda(item)();
  //If item is not a function,
  //lambda creates a function
  //then we return the result of that function
};
```

When you'll use it: Basically, $lambda saves you the time of figuring out if a value is a function that returns a value or if it's just a value. It's a subtle concept, and you may not find yourself using it.

$random :: Core/Core.js

What it does: $random returns a random number in a given range.

Usage:

```
$random(min, max)
```

Example:

```
var mortalKombat = {
  contestants: [Scorpion, Sub-Zero, Ermac, Smoke,
    Reptile, Noob Saibot, Rain],
  play: function(player){
    //The player fights a random opponent
    player.fight(
      $random(0, mortalKombat.contestants.length-1)
    );
  }
};
```

When you'll use it: This is pretty straightforward. $random just gives you a random number.

$time :: Core/Core.js

What it does: $time returns the current time as a timestamp (an integer).

Usage:

```
$time()
```

Example:

```
var ninja = {
  lastFight: 0,
  fight: function(enemy){
    //Is the ninja too tired?
    if ($time() - ninja.lastFight < 1000) return;
    //No! Fight!!!
    enemy.isAlive = false;
    ninja.lastFight = $time();
  }
};
```

When you'll use it: $time can be used for a lot of things. Basically, it's just a shortcut to new Date().getTime(), and it returns a large integer. You can use it to measure the duration between events or to generate a number that is unique for an event (provided you don't have events firing at a rate faster than one per millisecond).

$try :: Core/Core.js

What it does: $try will attempt to execute any number of functions, returning either the return value of the first one that does not throw an error or null if none of them succeed.

Usage:

```
$try (fn, fn, fn, etc.);
```

Example:

```
var result = $try(function(){
    return some.made.up.object;
    //Fails - this is nonsense
}, function(){
    return jibberish.that.doesnt.exist;
    //More junk, throws errors
}, function(){
    return 2+2;
}); //result == 4
```

When you'll use it: $try is just another shortcut to save a little time. It's a functional programming way of looking at try/catch that basically does the same thing, except you can run numerous functions through it.

Browser: Information About the Client

MooTools contains a set of useful shortcuts to information about the visitor's browser. All the engine detection is feature based (rather than sniffing the client string, which is unreliable). There's not a lot to explain here, so I'll just quote the documentation. You can reference this information by referring directly to the attribute.

Example:

```
if(Browser.Engine.trident4) {
    alert('Hey, IE6 was released in 2001! UPGRADE!');
}
```

Features:

- `Browser.Features.xpath`: (Boolean) true if the browser supports DOM queries using XPath

- `Browser.Features.xhr`: (Boolean) true if the browser supports the native XMLHTTP object

Engine:

- `Browser.Engine.trident`: (Boolean) True if the current browser is Internet Explorer (any version)

- `Browser.Engine.trident4`: (Boolean) True if the current browser is Internet Explorer 6

- `Browser.Engine.trident5`: (Boolean) True if the current browser is Internet Explorer 7

- `Browser.Engine.gecko`: (Boolean) True if the current browser is Mozilla/Gecko

- `Browser.Engine.webkit`: (Boolean) True if the current browser is Safari/Konqueror

- `Browser.Engine.webkit419`: (Boolean) True if the current browser is Safari 2/WebKit prior to and including version 419

- `Browser.Engine.webkit420`: (Boolean) True if the current browser is Safari 3 (WebKit SVN Build)/WebKit after version 419

- `Browser.Engine.presto`: (Boolean) True if the current browser is Opera

- `Browser.Engine.name`: (String) The name of the engine

Platform:

- `Browser.Platform.mac`: (Boolean) True if the platform is Mac

- `Browser.Platform.windows`: (Boolean) True if the platform is Windows

- `Browser.Platform.linux`: (Boolean) True if the platform is Linux

- `Browser.Platform.other`: (Boolean) True if the platform is neither Mac, Windows, nor Linux

- `Browser.Platform.name`: (String) The name of the platform

Chapter 4: Native Objects

JavaScript contains numerous native object types (`String`, `Array`, `Function`, `Boolean`, `Element`, etc.) that in many ways leave a lot to be desired. What's more, different browsers implement these objects differently, making it difficult to write code that works across them all without a lot of conditionals sniffing for different browsers.

MooTools implements functionality into the native objects to make them both easier to work with (by adding shortcut methods) and more reliable (by doing all the browser sniffing for you and providing you with a single API that works for all browsers). These methods should always be used rather than their native counterparts. MooTools will not only help you deal with browser inconsistencies, but also protect you against things like memory leaks. For more on this, see "Why You Should Use a JavaScript Framework" in the Introduction.

Native.implement

In addition to altering these native objects, MooTools also allows you to change them yourself. If there's a method you wish `String` or `Array` had, you can easily add it. The syntax is very similar to how `implement` works with classes. Here's an example:

```
String.implement({
  alert: function(){alert(this);},
  log: function(){console.log(this);}
});
"foo".alert() //Alerts "foo"
"foo".log() //Logs "foo"
```

The `implement` method for both `Class` and `Native` work the same—they alter the prototype of all the objects of that type. So the preceding example doesn't add the methods `log` and `alert` to a specific string, it adds it to all of them by modifying the parent—the prototype of all strings.

This chapter will dig into the native objects:

- `Array`*
- `Object` (a.k.a. `Hash`)
- `Function`*
- `Number`*
- `String`*
- `Event`
- `Element`

For the items marked with an asterisk (*), you should use the literal declarations for each. For example:

```
var numbers = [1,2,3]; //Yes
var numbers = new Array(1,2,3); //No
```

The exceptions are `Event`, `Element`, and `Hash`. For `Hash`, in particular, you should use literal declarations for objects, but you'll need to initialize those objects into a `Hash` if you want to use the `Hash` methods:

```
//This is a standard object
var fruits = {
  apple: 'red',
  lemon: 'yellow',
  grape: 'purple'
};
//Here is the same object as a hash:
var fruits = new Hash({
  apple: 'red',
  lemon: 'yellow',
```

```
  grape: 'purple'
});
fruits.each(function(color, fruit){
  alert(fruit + 's are ' + color);
  //Alerts apples are red, lemons are yellow, etc.
});
```

So even objects are declared as literals and only initialized as `Hash` instances if you want the methods of `Hash` applied to them (see more in "Objects (a.k.a. *Hash*)" later in this chapter).

Arrays

The native `Array` prototype gets a lot of love in MooTools. Arrays don't require any instantiation to acquire these methods (unless you're working with an iterable object that isn't a true `Array`, like the `arguments` object— see "Iterable Helpers and Shortcuts: *$arguments, $each, $splat, $A,* and *$H*" in Chapter 3). This means you can (and should) use the literal initialization for arrays. For example:

```
var numbers = [1,2,3];
numbers.each(function(value){
  alert(value);
  //Alerts 1, 2, 3
});
```

Array Methods

Arrays have numerous native methods (`push`, `slice`, `pop`, etc.), but not all of these are easy to use, and many of them leave something to be desired. In some cases, methods appear to have just been left out, like `indexOf`, which is not in the original JavaScript 1.0 specification. It is, however, in the 1.5 specification, which many modern browsers implement (Firefox, Safari, Opera, etc.). MooTools adds numerous methods to `Array`. Most of these are the methods defined in the 1.5 specification, and, for browsers that already support these methods natively, MooTools doesn't alter them.

For older browsers that don't support them, MooTools adds them so that you can use them safely without having to worry whether they are present.

Here's a quick rundown of all the `Array` methods:

METHOD TYPE	METHOD NAME
Iteration	`each, filter, some, every, map`
Introspection	`indexOf, getLast, getRandom`
Manipulation	`erase, extend, include, combine,` `associate, clean, flatten`
Less commonly used	`rgbToHex, link`

Array :: Iteration Methods

The most used methods on `Array` will no doubt be employed to iterate over thier properties. All of the iteration methods have the following in common:

- They take two arguments: a function to execute for each item in the array and an optional object to which that function should be bound.
- The function passed as the first argument is passed two arguments: the item for that iteration and the index of it.

Let's look at `each`, which you'll use the most.

Array.each

What it does: Iterates over each item in an array and executes a method for each item. The method is passed as arguments the value and the index of that value in the array. `Array.each` takes an optional second argument for an object to which to bind the passed-in method.

Usage:

```
myArray.each(function, bind);
```

Example:
```
[1,2,3].each(function(value, index){
  alert('the item at position ' + index +
      ' is ' + value);
  //Alerts "the item at position 0 is 1",
  //"...1 is 2", etc.
});
```

When you'll use it: Using `each` instead of a `for` loop allows for a more functional approach to your code (see "Functional Programming" in the Appendix), but it also can make your code less verbose and easier to manage.

The ability to bind something to that function is of course useful (see "'this' and Binding" in the Appendix), and note that you *don't* have to use `.bind` on the function. For example:

```
//Incorrect
[1,2,3].each(function(value, index){}.bind(someObject));
//Correct
[1,2,3].each(function(value, index){}, someObject);
```

Also note that you don't have to declare the `index` argument for the function passed in if you aren't making use of it. There's no expense in declaring it though, it just saves a few characters if you don't need it.

```
//Here, index is unused
[1,2,3].each(function(value, index){alert(value);});

//I don't need index in my method, so there's
//no point in declaring it
[1,2,3].each(function(value){alert(value);});
```

The same is true for the bind object. If the contents of the method that you pass to `each` do not make a reference to `this`, there's no point in binding the function to an object. Although there's no real expense for doing it anyway, there's no benefit.

Anonymous Methods vs. Named Functions

The preceding examples use an anonymous function, but there's no reason why you can't pass the method a function that's already defined. Consider the following:

```
var say = function(msg) {alert(msg);};
[1,2,3].each(say); //Alerts 1, 2, 3
[1,2,3].each(function(msg){alert(msg);}); //Same thing
```

Other Iteration Methods

So each lets you iterate over the objects in an array, but what of the other methods? So long as you understand how each works, you can apply the same methodology to the other iteration methods. Here's what they do:

Array.filter: This method returns a new array excluding items for which the method passed to filter return something "falsy" (zero, empty string, null, undefined, or false).

```
var evens = [1,2,3,4,5].filter(function(value, index){
   return !(value % 2);
}); //Returns [2,4]
```

Array.some: This method returns a Boolean—true if the method passed to some returns true at least once.

```
var atLeastOneOfTheseIsBiggerThanTwo = [1,2,3].some(
   function(value, index){
      return value > 2;
   }
); //Returns true because 3 > 2
var oneIsEven = [1,3,5].some(function(value) {
   return value % 2 == 0;
}); //Returns false, because 1,3,5 are each not even
```

Array.every: This method returns a Boolean—true if the method passed to every returns true for each item in the array.

```
var greaterThanOne = function(val){ return val > 1 };
var lessThanFive = function(val) { return val < 5 };
[1,2,3].every(greaterThanOne); //Returns false
[1,2,3].every(lessThanFive); //Returns true
```

`Array.map`: This method returns a new array—the result of the returned values for the method passed to `map`.

```
var timesTwo = function(value){
  return value*2;
};
var twoFourSix = [1,2,3].map(timesTwo);
var timesThree = [1,2,3].map(
  function(value){return value*3}
);
```

Array :: Introspection Methods

The following shortcut methods are mostly used for introspection. For instance, `indexOf` doesn't alter the array or iterate over it, it just returns the index of an item in the array.

`Array.indexOf`: This method returns the index of an item in the array.

```
[0,1,2,3].indexOf(3); //Returns 4
```

`Array.getLast`: This method returns the last item in the array.

```
[0,1,2,3].getLast(); //Returns 3
```

`Array.getRandom`: This method gets a random item from the array.

```
[0,1,2,3].getRandom(); //Returns a random value
```

Array :: Manipulation Methods

Finally, you have the methods that alter the array. As noted earlier, JavaScript already has numerous methods for doing this, including `splice`, `unshift`, `pop`, `push`, and so forth. MooTools adds a few more to your toolbox. All of these methods return the array to you, but in the case of erase, empty, and include, the array is also altered. So, for example, myArray.erase(foo) alters myArray.

Array.erase: This method erases an item from the array.

```
['ninja', 'samurai', 'ninja'].erase('ninja')
//Returns ['samurai']
var warriors = ['ninja', 'samurai', 'ninja'];
warriors.erase('ninja'); //warriors = ['samurai']

//When an item is not found the array is unaltered
['shuriken', 'nunchucks', 'darts'].erase('katana')
//Returns ['shuriken', 'nunchucks', 'darts']
```

Array.empty: This method removes all the items from the array.

```
var foo = [1,2,3];
foo.empty(); //foo.length == 0
```

Array.extend: This method adds all the items in one array to the other (allows duplicates).

```
var foo = [1,2,3];
foo.extend([2,3,4]; //foo = [1,2,3,2,3,4]
```

Array.include: This method pushes the value into the array if it's not already present.

```
['ninja', 'samurai'].include('kung-foo master')
//Returns ['ninja', 'samurai', 'kung-foo master']
['ninja', 'samurai'].include('ninja')
//Returns ['ninja', 'samurai']
var warriors = ['ninja', 'samurai'];
warriors.include('kung-foo master');
//warriors = ['ninja', 'samurai', 'kung-foo master']
```

All of the following methods return a new array to you:

Array.combine: This method combines two arrays without duplicates. Note that combine will exclude any duplicates found in the array passed in.

```
['ninja', 'samurai'].combine(['ninja',
 'kung-foo  master'])
//Returns ['ninja', 'samurai', 'kung-foo master']
```

Array.associate: This method returns an object of keys/values where the passed-in array becomes the keys.

```
['good', 'evil'].associate(['samurai', 'ninja']);
//Returns {samurai: 'good', ninja: 'evil'}
```

Array.clean: This method is a shortcut to a version of Array.filter that simply returns the value as its condition.

```
[null, 0, "", false, true].filter(function(value){
   return value;
});
//Returns [true], as all the other values are "falsy"
[null, 0, "" , false, true].clean(); //Same result
```

Array.flatten: This method flattens an array of arrays into a single array, returning a new array.

```
var myArray = [1,2,3,[4,5, [6,7]], [[[8]]]];
var newArray = myArray.flatten();
//newArray is [1,2,3,4,5,6,7,8]
```

Objects (a.k.a. *Hash*)

JavaScript has a basic object type—a hash or map—for storing values in a single memory space. The language extends this very basic object for nearly all the other types in the library, so, for example, a function is also an object.

Unlike other natives in the language, MooTools does not extend the object prototype to add helper methods, and neither should you. This is due to the way you iterate over the items in an object. Here's what it looks like in plain vanilla JavaScript:

```
var ninja = {
   weapon: 'sword',
   equipment: 'rope'
};
for (var prop in ninja){
   alert("The ninja's " + prop + " is a " + ninja[prop]);
}
```

This example will send an alert that the ninja has a sword and a rope. However, if you extend the object prototype, you would get those properties too. Because this affects every type of object, it's considered forbidden—a no-no.

But working with objects is something developers do often in JavaScript, and it's a hassle to not have the same kind of helper methods that MooTools offers for the other native types. To remedy this situation, MooTools offers the Hash class. By instantiating this class with an object, you get a new item that contains the properties of your object and the helper methods.

This means that if you want to add methods to an object, you must initialize it as a special extended type of object, and that's what Hash does. When you invoke new Hash(object), you are returned a copy of the object, but now it has new properties—methods that you can use to manage and inspect the data in the object.

Hash

What it does: Extends the native object (as in {foo: bar}) in JavaScript to add iteration methods.

Core.js declares the Hash class specifically for the iteration method each because it's used in other scripts in the library, and so it has to be defined in `Core.js`. But because `Hash` is used liberally in MooTools, you'll likely include `Native/Hash.js` in any code you write.

Usage:

```
new Hash({foo: 'bar'});
$H({foo: 'bar'}); //$H is just a shortcut for new Hash
```

Example:

```
var ninjas = new Hash({
  red: {side: 'unknown'},
  black: {side: 'evil'},
  white: {side: 'good'}
});
ninjas.each(function(value, key){
  alert(key + ' ninja is on the side of ' + value.side);
});
```

When you'll use it: `Hash` extends a native JavaScript object to add methods to it that can be used to manage its data and to iterate over it.

$H

What it does: Serves as a shortcut for `new Hash()`.

Usage:

```
var myHash = $H({foo: 'bar'});
//Same as
var myHash = new Hash({foo: 'bar'});
```

Hash Methods

MooTools adds numerous methods to objects when you include `Native/Hash.js`, but `Core/Core.js` only adds the few that are required for everything in the library to work. Given how widely used it is, you'll likely have `Hash.js` in your library.

Much like the `Array` methods, the `Hash` methods, listed here, are mostly used for iteration and introspection:

METHOD TYPE	METHOD NAME
Iteration	each, filter, some, every, map
Introspection	has, keyOf, hasValue, toQueryString, get, getClean, getKeys, getLength, getValues
Manipulation	set, extend, combine, erase, empty, include

Hash :: Iteration Methods

`Hash` has all of the same iteration methods that `Array` uses, and they work exactly the same way with one distinction: the function passed to the method does not receive the **value and the index** but instead the **value and the key**. Let's look at `Hash.each`:

Hash.each

What it does: Lets you iterate over each member of a hash and perform a function for each item, much like `Array.each`. The `bind` argument is optional (as with `Array.each`). The passed-in function will be executed for each item in the hash, and it will be passed as arguments the value and the key of that value in the hash.

Usage:

```
myHash.each(function(value, key){/*your code*/}, bind);
//bind is optional
```

Example:
```
//A conversation between two people arriving for work
$H({
  goodNinja: 'Ralph',
  evilNinja: 'Sam'
}).each(function(value, key) {
  alert(key + ': Morning ' + value + '.');
  //Alerts
  //"goodNinja: Morning Ralph. "
  //"evilNinja: Morning Sam. "
});
```

When you'll use it: Whenever you have an object of key/value pairs and need to iterate over them, it's easier to use `Hash.each` than it is to use a `for` loop. In addition to the easier syntax, you have the ability to define scope (with binding) and use closures (see "Closures," "Functional Programming (a.k.a. Lambda)," and "'this' and Binding" in the Appendix).

Tip   You can iterate quickly over an object without using `Hash` with `$each`:

```
$each(data, function(value, key) {...}[, bind]);
```

Using `$H.each` requires about the same effort:

```
$H(data).each(function(value, key{...}[,bind]);
```

All the other iteration methods for `Hash` follow this same pattern and do the same things they do for `Array`.

Other Iteration Methods

Using the same pattern as `Hash.each`, you can use these other iteration methods. As with `Hash.each`, each method here iterates over each member in the hash, applying the passed-in function to each member and passing that function the value and the key for each one. They also take a second, optional, argument for binding.

`Hash.filter`: This method returns a new `Hash` excluding any item for which the method passed to `filter` returns something "falsy" (zero, empty string, `null`, `undefined`, or `false`).

```
var evens = $H({
  a: 1, b: 2, c: 3
}).filter(function(value, key){
  return !(value % 2);
}); //evens = Hash({b: 2});
```

`Hash.some`: This method returns a Boolean—`true` if the method passed to `some` returns `true` at least once. Note that you don't have to declare the key in the passed function if you don't use it.

```
var oneIsEven = $H({
  a: 1, b: 3, c: 5
}).some(function(value) {
  return value % 2 == 0;
}); //Returns false, because 1,3,5 are each not even
```

`Hash.every`: This method returns a Boolean—`true` if the method passed to `every` returns `true` for each item in the hash.

```
var greaterThanOne = function(value){return value > 1};
var lessThanFive = function(value) {return value < 5};
$H({a: 1, b: 2, c:3}).every(greaterThanOne);
//Returns false
$H({a: 1, b: 2, c:3}).every(lessThanFive);
//Returns true
```

`Hash.map`: This method returns a new hash—the result of the returned values for the method passed to `map`.

```
var timesTwo = function(value){
  return value*2;
};
var twoFourSix = $H({a: 1, b: 2, c: 3}).map(timesTwo);
//twoFourSix = Hash({a: 2, b: 4, c: 6});
var timesThree = $H({
  a: 1, b: 2, c: 3
}).map(function(value, index){
  return value*3
});
//timesThree =  Hash({a: 3, b: 6, c: 9});
```

Hash :: Introspection Methods

`Hash` provides methods to retrieve information about the data in the hash that should be used instead of the dot notation or bracket notation used in native objects.

```
var ninja = {color: "black", side: "evil"};
ninja.color = "red";
//This is OK for native objects of course
var ninjaHash = new Hash(ninja);
ninjaHash.get('color') ;
//Returns "red"
```

`Hash.get`: This method returns the value for the given key.

```
$H({apple: 'red', lemon: 'yellow'}).get("apple");
//Returns 'red'
$H({apple: 'red', lemon: 'yellow'}).get("grape");
//Returns undefined
```

Note   Hash.get does not retrieve properties of Hash—only the properties of the object you pass in to Hash. So, for example, although Hash has the method each, invoking $H({foo: bar}).get('each') would return null; this is because each is not a member of {foo:bar}— it's a member of Hash. Hash wraps your object with its own methods, but it treats your object as if Hash has not altered it.

Hash.getClean: This method returns an object that has none of the hash methods.

```
$H({apple: 'red', lemon: 'yellow'}).getClean;
//Returns {apple: 'red', lemon: 'yellow'}
```

Hash.getKeys: This method returns an array of all the keys in the hash.

```
$H({apple: 'red', lemon: 'yellow'}).getKeys();
//Returns ["apple", "lemon"]
```

Hash.getLength: This method returns the length of the number of key/value objects in the hash.

```
$H({apple: 'red', lemon: 'yellow'}).getLength();
//Returns 2
```

Hash.getValues: This method returns an array of all the keys in the hash.

```
$H({apple: 'red', lemon: 'yellow'}).getValues();
//Returns ['red', 'yellow']
```

Hash.has: This method returns true if the hash has a value for the specified key.

```
$H({apple: 'red', lemon: 'yellow'}).has('grape');
//Returns false
$H({apple: 'red', lemon: 'yellow'}).has('apple');
//Returns true
```

`Hash.hasValue`: This method returns `true` if the hash contains the specified value.

```
$H({apple: 'red', lemon: 'yellow'}).has('red');
//Returns true
$H({apple: 'red', lemon: 'yellow'}).has('purple');
// Returns false
```

`Hash.keyOf`: This method returns the corresponding key for a given value if the hash contains that value.

```
$H({apple: 'red', lemon: 'yellow'}).keyOf('red');
//Returns 'apple'
$H({apple: 'red', lemon: 'yellow'}).keyOf('purple');
//Undefined
```

`Hash.toQueryString`: This method returns a query string of key/value pairs for all the contents of the hash. Note that this really only works if the `toString` method of the values returns a useful notation of the object. So, for instance, if one of the values in your hash is a DOM element, the `toString` representation of that is not likely to be useful. Booleans, strings, numbers, and arrays are more likely to be useful with this method.

```
$H({apple: 'red', lemon: 'yellow'}).toQueryString();
//Returns apple=red&lemon=yellow
```

Hash :: Manipulation Methods

`Hash` has several methods that allow you to alter the contents of the hash itself.

`Hash.empty`: This method removes all key/value pairs from the object.

```
$H({apple: 'red', lemon: 'yellow'}).empty();
//Hash no longer has any keys/values
```

`Hash.erase`: This method removes a specific key/value pair (pass in the key).

```
$H({apple: 'red', lemon: 'yellow'}).erase('apple');
//Hash is now {lemon: 'yellow'}
```

`Hash.extend`: This method adds all the key/values for the object passed in, **overwriting** any namespace collisions. This is the equivalent syntax for `$extend(obj1, obj2)`.

```
$H({
  apple: 'red', lemon: 'yellow'
}).extend({apple: 'green'});
//Hash is now {apple: 'green', lemon: 'yellow'}
```

`Hash.include`: This method adds the key/value set if the key is not already present.

```
$H({
  apple: 'red', lemon: 'yellow'
}).include('apple', 'green');
//Hash is now {apple: 'red', lemon: 'yellow'};
```

`Hash.combine`: This method adds all the key/values for the object passed in, **excluding** any namespace collisions.

```
$H({apple: 'red', lemon: 'yellow'}).combine({
  apple: 'green', grape: 'purple'
});
//Hash is now
//{apple: 'red', lemon: 'yellow', grape: 'purple'}
```

`Hash.set`: This method sets the value for the given key.

```
$H({
  apple: 'red', lemon: 'yellow'
}).set('apple', 'green');
//Hash({apple: 'green', lemon: 'yellow'});
```

Functions

At the heart of modern JavaScript is the concept of functional programming (see "Functional Programming (a.k.a. Lambda)" in the Appendix). Unfortunately, there are a lot of things that you'll likely want to accomplish with functions that the native JavaScript specification makes far from simple. Thankfully, MooTools makes most of these tasks easier to accomplish.

Function Methods Generate Copies

As with most native objects, MooTools adds methods to the `Function` prototype. This makes these methods available on all functions. It's important to note that executing *most* of these methods *returns a new function* (some of them return the result of invoking the function, like `$try` or `.call`). The new function is the same as the old one, except some new attribute has been defined for this new one, *but it's not the same function—* it's a copy of it.

This distinction is important to keep in mind whenever you have a pointer to a function and you need to reference it again.

An example here requires that I jump ahead a bit, but I think it's important, so bear with me. Consider adding an event to a DOM element (this is MooTools syntax):

```
var highlight = function(){
  this.setStyle('background-color', 'yellow'
});
$('myElement').addEvent('click',
  highlight.bind($('myElement').getParent())
);
//...Later
$('myElement').removeEvent('click', highlight);
//This won't work!
```

Allow me to explain the preceding code. It contains a method that will change the background color of an element to yellow. It references the keyword `this`, meaning that you expect an element to be bound to the function (see "'this' and Binding" in the Appendix). Then you attach an event to an element, but you bind the `highlight` method to the parent of your element because you want to highlight that. Later you decide to remove that event. `removeEvent` takes as its argument the event (`click`) and the function you attached previously (`highlight`).

But wait! This won't work! Why? Because when you called `bind` on `highlight` when you attached the event, what was attached was a copy of `highlight`—a copy with its `bind` property set.

So how do you manage this kind of scenario? You have to keep a reference to the new copy:

```
var highlight = function(){
  this.setStyle('background-color', 'yellow')
};
var parentHighlight =
  highlight.bind($('myElement').getParent());
$('myElement').addEvent('click', parentHighlight);
//...Later
$('myElement').removeEvent('click', parentHighlight);
//voila!
```

This pattern isn't one you'll encounter a lot—needing to keep a reference like this—but it's very important to recognize that when you call a method on a function, it *usually* returns a copy of the function. The methods that do *not* return a copy like this are the methods that return something other than the function—like `attempt`, which returns the `result` of the function or `null` if the attempt fails.

Function.attempt

This executes the function and returns the value that the function returns unless there is an exception, in which case it returns null; however, the exception is not raised to the browser. This takes an optional second argument for a bind object (see `Function.bind` next).

```
var say = function(msg){
  alert(msg.toString());
  return true;
};
say(null);
//This will throw an error as null.toString is undefined
var spoke = say.attempt(null);
//Will still fail, but will not raise an error
//spoke == null
```

Function.bind

This binds an object to the `this` keyword within the function; it takes an optional second argument for arguments to be passed to the function. If you use this second argument, you can pass in a single object or, if you wish to pass in more than one argument to the function, pass in an array.

```
myFunction.bind(object);
myFunction.bind(object, argument);
myFunction.bind(object, [arg1, arg2, etc.]);
```

For example:

```
var highlight = function(){
  this.setStyle('background-color', 'yellow');
};
var boundHighlight = highlight.bind($('myElement'));
boundHighlight();

//Here it is again using the args option
var highlight = function(color){
  this.setStyle('background-color', color);
};
var boundHighlight =
  highlight.bind($('myElement'), 'yellow');
boundHighlight();
```

```
//And here it is passing in more than one argument
var highlight = function(color, border) {
  this.setStyles({
    'background-color': color,
    'border-color': border
  });
};
var boundHighlight =
  highlight.bind($('myElement'), ['red', 'green']);
boundHighlight();
```

At this point, you are no doubt asking yourself why you would ever write JavaScript this way. The reality is that you wouldn't in all likelihood. I'm trying to illustrate the concept of binding here so that when you get into the examples in the next section of the book, it'll be clear to you.

But to put it in perspective, by writing code this way, it is possible to write very abstract methods and collections of methods that can be reused in many, many different ways. Indeed, all you have to do is look through MooTools itself to see all of these concepts in action (see "'this' and Binding" in the Appendix for more details on binding).

Function.bindWithEvent

You probably won't find yourself using this very often, but it does sometimes come in handy. Here's what appears in the MooTools documentation: "Changes the scope of this within the target function to refer to the bind parameter. It also makes 'space' for an event. This allows the function to be used in conjunction with Element.addEvent and arguments." Here's the syntax:

```
myFunction.bindWithEvent(bind, arguments);
//arguments are optional
```

And here's an example:

```
function myFunc(event, add){
  //Note that 'this' here refers to the current
  //scope, typically the window, not an element.
  //We'll need to bind this function to the
  //element we want to alter.
  this.setStyle('top', event.client.x + add);
};
$(myElement).addEvent('click',
  myFunc.bindWithEvent(myElement, 100);
//When clicked, the element will move to the
//position of the mouse + 100.
```

The reason you won't use it very often is because you'll typically work with events via the element method addEvent, which automatically does all this for you.

Function.delay

This method delays the function, executing it after the given duration specified. This method returns the JavaScript timeout ID, which can be used to cancel the call. This takes as optional arguments bind and arguments; see the discussion on function.bind earlier in the chapter for more on these arguments.

```
var hilight = function(color){
  this.setStyle('background-color', color);
};
var hilightDelay =
  highlight.delay(500, $('myElement'), 'red');
//Wait 500ms, then execute highlight, passing 'red'
//as its argument binding $('myElement') to
//the function
$clear(hilightDelay); //Nevermind!
```

Function.pass

This method will create a copy of a function with its arguments already specified (to be executed later). The second argument for binding is optional (see the discussion on `function.bind` earlier).

```
var say = function(msg){
  alert(msg.toString());
  return true;
};
var howdy = say.pass('howdy');
//...Later
howdy(); //Alerts "howdy"
```

Function.periodical

This method works just like `function.delay`, except that it recurs.

```
var blink = function(){
  if (this.getStyle('display') == 'none')
    this.setStyle('display', 'block');
  else this.setStyle('display', 'none');
};
blink.periodical(500, $('myElement'));
//Egads! The blink tag is back!
```

Function.run

JavaScript has its own native methods to execute a function while binding something to it at the same time: `Function.apply` and `Function.call`. Those methods take as arguments the `this` keyword to bind to the function and a second, optional list of arguments to pass to the function. The difference between them is that `call` takes a single argument, while `apply` takes an array.

For example:

```
var highlight = function(color){
  this.setStyle('background-color', color);
};
highlight.apply($('myElement'), ['yellow']);
//Same as
highlight.call($('myElement'), 'yellow');
```

This is handy if you need to bind something to a function before you execute it. Otherwise, you'd have to do something silly like this:

```
highlight.bind($('myElement'), 'yellow')();
```

What if you want to just run a method and pass arguments to it but not necessarily bind anything to it? What if you want to call a function and pass it an array of arguments? It's ugly to pass null values in for the bind argument just to be able to pass an array to the function:

```
var say = function(name, msg){
  alert(name + ' says ' + msg);
};
var words = ['bob','hi'];
say.apply(null, words);
//We don't need to bind anything,
//but passing null is kinda ugly
```

So MooTools gives you function.run, which takes as its first argument an array *or* a single object to pass to the function, and the bind argument is optional.

```
var say = function(msg){ alert(msg); };
var talk = function(){
  $A(arguments).each(say);
};
talk('I', 'like', 'cheese'); //Alerts each argument
var msgs = ['I', 'like', 'cheese'];
talk.run(msgs);
```

OK, why not just pass the arguments straight to the function—why would you want to pass an array of arguments? Well, sometimes you are getting values programmatically, and you have the arguments for a function as a reference to an array or a string or whatever. You can throw any of these things at run, and it'll handle it.

Numbers

Most of the native methods for Number in JavaScript are part of the Math object or are stand-alone functions. For example, parseInt is just a built-in function to parse a string to an integer.

This isn't a very MooTools way of doing things though; MooTools prefers to add methods to the prototypes of natives, so MooTools translates most of these as methods on Number.

As a result, most of the MooTools methods for Number are native methods just applied to the numbers as methods.

```
var x = 3.5;
x.floor(); //Returns 3
Math.floor(3.5); //Same thing
```

Note that you can't execute these methods on the literal for numbers (because number literals can contain decimals), so this won't work:

```
3.floor();
```

But this would:

```
(3).floor();
```

In addition to converting all the Math methods (abs, acos, asin, atan, atan2, ceil, cos, exp, floor, log, max, min, pow, sin, sqrt, and tan) to native methods, MooTools adds the following methods:

`Number.limit`: This method limits the number between two bounds.

```
(12).limit(2, 6.5);   //Returns 6.5
(-4).limit(2, 6.5);   //Returns 2
(4.3).limit(2, 6.5); //Returns 4.3
```

`Number.round`: This method rounds a number to a given precision.

```
(12.45).round()    //Returns 12
(12.45).round(1)   //Returns 12.5
(12.45).round(-1) //Returns 10
```

`Number.times`: This method iterates a method a given number of times, passing as the argument the number of the current iteration. It also takes an optional second argument for binding.

```
(4).times(alert);
//Alerts "0", then "1", then "2", then "3".
```

In many ways, this is just a shortcut for a standard `for` loop, but it also conforms to that notion of functional programming discussed elsewhere in this book.

`Number.toFloat`: This method returns a number as a float. This is useful because sometimes you have a value and you may not know whether it's a string or a number (for example, `Element.setStyle` takes for the numerical property of CSS values either a number or a string).

```
(111).toFloat(); //Returns 111
(111.1).toFloat(); //Returns 111.1
```

`Number.toInt`: Much like `Number.toFloat`, this is useful when you have a variable that may be a number or a string. It takes as an optional argument a base value that defaults to `10`. This is an important distinction to the native `parseInt`, which also defaults to `10` unless the string you pass it starts with a zero; in that case, it switches to octal for the radix so that `parseInt(012)` returns `10` (awesome!), unless you pass it a second argument to explicitly tell it to use base 10, as it would otherwise . . . But I digress. MooTools adds `Number.toInt` and makes this all better.

```
"111".toInt(); //Returns 111
(111.1).toInt(); //Returns 111
"012".toInt(); //Returns 12
//You can specify a different base; this returns 7:
"111".toInt(2);
```

Strings

Strings in MooTools get several methods that fall into two basic camps:
introspection and manipulation (the bulk of them are in the latter):

METHOD TYPE	METHOD NAME
Introspection	`contains, test`
Manipulation	`capitalize, camelCase, clean, escapeRegExp, hyphenate, stripScripts, substitute, toFloat, toInt, trim`
Less commonly used	`hexToRgb, rgbToHex`

`String.contains`: This method checks to see whether the string contains
the passed-in string. You can pass in a second argument, which it will use to
separate the string into chunks, and then compare each of those to the one
you're looking for.

```
'a bc'.contains('bc'); //Returns true
'a b c'.contains('c', ' '); //Returns true
'a bc'.contains('b', ' '); //Returns false
```

`String.test`: This method checks to see whether a string passes a regular
expression; it returns `true` or `false`. You can pass a second argument for
`RegExp` options. Alternatively, you can pass in a `RegExp` object.

```
"I like cookies".test("cookie"); //Returns true
"I like cookies".test("COOKIE", "i");
 //Returns true (ignore case)
"I like cookies".test(/COOKIE/i); //Same as above
"I like cookies".test("cake"); //Returns false
```

`String.toFloat`, `String.toInt`: These methods convert a value to a float or an integer.

```
"3".toInt(); //Returns 3
"3.4".toInt(); //Returns 3
"3.4".toFloat(); //Returns 3.4
```

`String.camelCase`, `String.hyphenate`: These two methods convert strings between each other.

```
"borderTop".hyphenate(); //Returns "border-top"
"border-top".camelCase(); //Returns "borderTop"
```

`String.capitalize`: This method capitalizes the first letter of each word.

```
"i like cookies".toInt(); //Returns I Like Cookies
```

`String.trim`, `String.clean`: This method removes whitespace at the beginning and end of a string; `clean` also removes line breaks.

```
" i    like      cookies   \n\n".clean();
//Returns "i like cookies"
```

`String.escapeRegExp`: This method escapes the characters in a string that would otherwise mess up a regular expression.

```
'animals.sheep[1]'.escapeRegExp();
//Returns 'animals\.sheep\[1\]'
```

`String.stripScripts`: This method removes all `<script>` tags from a string of HTML; you can optionally pass in `true` as the argument to evaluate those scripts before removing them.

`String.substitute`: This method substitutes keywords in a string using an object of key/values. You can optionally pass in a `RegExp` as the second argument to denote the pattern used to match the keys. The default for this is `/\?{((^}]+)}/g`, which translates to "{key}".

```
var myString =
   "{subject} just {property_1} to be  {property_2}.";
 var myObject = {
   subject: 'Lonely ninja',
   property_1: 'wants',
   property_2: 'friends'
 };
 myString.substitute(myObject);
 //Lonely ninja just wants to be friends.
```

Events

JavaScript is mostly about interactivity. The next chapter explores the native DOM element and the methods used to monitor them for clicks and drags and other events. When a user interacts with a DOM element, the browser fires events for each interaction—mouseover, click, and so on.

Methods applied to these events are executed when they occur and are passed a native Event object. This object contains information about that event that is often very useful. Additionally, the event has methods that can be executed to prevent the default behavior from continuing. For example, you can monitor the submit event on a form and prevent the form from submitting by stopping the event.

Unfortunately, different browsers implement this object in different ways. MooTools unifies all these disparate objects into a single one with attributes and methods that are easier to use and understand.

Event Methods

Events only have three methods, and they all basically in some way or another obstruct the event from processing the way it normally would. To understand this requires knowledge of how DOM events are handled by browsers.

When an event fires on a DOM element, in some circumstances two primary things occur: the default behavior (clicking a link takes you to another page, clicking the submit button submits the form) and also propagation. Propagation occurs when you click (or mouseover, keydown, etc.) an element inside another element. The browser fires the `click` event for both elements, which makes sense, if you think about it: if you click a box inside a box, the browser doesn't really know which one you're really clicking—you're clicking both—so it fires the `onclick` event of the innermost element, and then its parent, and on up to the `document`.

MooTools provide methods to stop either or both of these actions:

`Event.preventDefault`: This prevents the default behavior from occurring.

```
$('myCheckbox').addEvent('click', function(event){
  event.preventDefault();
  //Will prevent the check box from being "checked".
});
```

Here the check box won't get checked, but if there's any other click behavior on this element or any of its parents, those events will fire.

`Element.stopPropagation`: This method prevents the events that fire on the parents of an element. For example, clicking an element will fire the `onclick` event for that element, and then the `onclick` event for its parent, and its parent's parent, and so on. `Element.stopPropagation` prevents these events from firing on the parents.

```
$('myElement').addEvent('click', function(){
  alert('click');
  return false;
  //Equivalent to stopPropagation and preventDefault.
});
$('myChild').addEvent('click', function(event){
  event.stopPropagation();
  //This will prevent the event from bubbling up,
  //and so that the parent's click event won't fire.
});
```

`Element.stop`: This is the method I use 99% of the time. It basically stops both the propagation of the event *and* the default behavior.

HTML:

```
<a id="myAnchor" href="http://google.com/">Visit
 Google.com</a>
```

JavaScript:

```
$('myAnchor').addEvent('click', function(event){
  event.stop();
  //Prevents the browser from following the link.
  this.setText("Where do you think you're going?");
  //'this' is Element that fires the Event.
});
```

Event Properties

In addition to the methods to prevent events from continuing, the `Event` object contains data about the event.

- `shift`: (Boolean) `true` if the user pressed the Shift key.

- `control`: (Boolean) `true` if the user pressed the Ctrl key.

- `alt`: (Boolean) `true` if the user pressed the Alt key.

- `meta`: (Boolean) `true` if the user pressed the meta key.

- `wheel`: (Integer) The amount of third button scrolling.

- `code`: (Integer) The keycode of the key pressed.
- `page.x`: (Integer) The x position of the mouse, relative to the full window.
- `page.y`: (Integer) The y position of the mouse, relative to the full window.
- `client.x`: (Integer) The x position of the mouse, relative to the viewport.
- `client.y`: (Integer) The y position of the mouse, relative to the viewport.
- `key`: (String) The key pressed as a lowercase string. `key` can be "enter", "up", "down", "left", "right", "space", "backspace", "delete", "esc", "a", "b", "c", "d", and so on.
- `target`: (Element) The event target, not extended with $ for performance reasons.
- `relatedTarget`: (Element) The event-related target, not extended with $.

The data about the event can let you author complex interactions, like using Ctrl+S to save a form or altering a CSS property for a DOM element when users scroll their mousewheel.

Chapter 5: Elements

Browsers implement what is known as the DOM—the Document Object Model. JavaScript as a language isn't indigenous to browsers nor limited to them, it's just that the browsers are where developers typically use JavaScript. But the browsers themselves extend the basic language to add methods and properties to JavaScript objects that relate to HTML tags rendered to the viewer.

This relationship between the JavaScript world and the HTML world is the DOM. With the DOM comes numerous methods that only make sense in a browser, and most of these are methods on `Element`, the JavaScript object that relates to HTML tags in the page. The methods that are natively part of `Element`, much like other native JavaScript methods, leave something to be desired. Often they seem overly verbose or explicit, while other times they seem woefully insufficient to allow for the authoring of clean code.

At its heart, MooTools really makes two things its priority: first, it strives to make writing object-oriented, reusable, and cleanly readable JavaScript an easy thing to do, and second, it strives to make interactive web pages easy to author. Consequently, MooTools gives a lot of attention to the `Element` native, adding many, many methods that allow you to write clean, legible, expressive code.

Creating and Cloning Elements

MooTools makes the task of creating an element much easier than native JavaScript, offering up a syntax that feels much like that for instantiating a class:

```
var myImg = new Element('img', {
  src: '/foo.jpg',
  alt: 'this is foo',
  //class is a reserved word in JS,
  //so we must use quotes
  'class': 'fooClass',
  //In addition to basic attributes,
  //you can declare special ones:
  events: {
    click: function(){ alert('click!');}
  },
  styles: {
    border: '1px solid blue',
    marginTop: '10px'
  },
  etc...
});
```

Note   Creating a new element doesn't inject it into the DOM. You can attach events to it and change its styles and properties, but for it to show up in the browser, you must inject it into the DOM. See the section "Element Injection and Removal" later in this chapter.

You can also clone elements. Doing so does not clone any events attached to that element, and by default it clones the children of the element, too. It also by default removes any IDs from the element (which according to standards should always be unique).

```
var myCopy = myElement.clone();
//This copies children
var myCopy_NoChildren = myElement.clone(false);
//Copies children and IDs
var myCopy_ChildrenAndIds = myElement.clone(true, true);
```

If you need to also clone events, that's a different method entirely (in `Element/Element.Events.js`):

```
var myCopy = myElement.clone();
//Clone the click events
myCopy.cloneEvents(myElement, 'click');
//Clone all of the events
myCopy.cloneEvents(myElement);
```

Of course, creating and injecting elements into the DOM is only a small part of the picture. You're much more likely to write most of your HTML the old fashioned way, and that means you must collect the elements from the document somehow.

Collecting Elements from the DOM

MooTools contains three shortcuts for collecting elements from the DOM: $, $$, and $E.

$ :: Element/Element.js

What it does: Collects an element from the DOM by ID.

Usage:

```
$('myElementId');
```

Example:

```
$('ninja').setStyle('visibility', 'hidden');
```

When you'll use it: The $ function has two main purposes:

- Serves as a shortcut for `document.getElementById`, which we can all agree is so many keystrokes that it's just cruel considering how often we need to perform the task
- Initializes element objects with MooTools

While it's possible to still collect elements by ID using the standard method (`document.getElementById`), it's a bad practice to use it when using

MooTools for a couple reasons: it's just more characters than using the MooTools method ($), and MooTools ensures that the element returned has had the MooTools element methods applied to it (see the next section).

Also note that any of the DOM collection methods (`Element.getElements`, for example) will initialize the elements returned.

Using $ to Ensure You Have an Initialized Element

This function is also useful when you aren't sure whether the value you have is a reference to an element or its ID, or if you are unsure whether that element has already been initialized for MooTools. For example, if you have a method or a function that accepts an element as an argument, the user might pass you an ID, an initialized element, or an element that hasn't yet been initialized. You can use $ as a quick way to ensure that you get an initialized element.

If you pass an argument to $ that is not an ID of an element in the DOM or isn't an element reference, it returns `null`, so it's also useful to check whether the ID of an element is found in the DOM or not. Consider the following demonstration:

```
function hideNinja(element) {
    element = $(element);
    if (element) element.setStyle('visibility', 'hidden');
};
```

In this example, the user could pass an ID (a string), an element that was collected already using $, or an element collected using non-MooTools means (`document.getElementById`). The $ function will return the initialized element or `false` if it can't locate the element in the DOM (if it's passed an ID; if you pass it an element, the element doesn't have to be in the DOM yet).

Using $ on an `Element` that's already been initialized does not have any ill effects or costs.

$$ :: Element/Element.js

What it does: Returns a collection of elements that match the passed-in selector.

Usage:

```
$$('div'); //All the divs in the DOM
$$('a', 'b'); //All the anchor & bold elements
```

Note   Using $$ with more than one selector will return a collection with the results of each selector grouped (so $$('a', 'b') will be a collection with all the links followed by all the bold elements).

Example:

```
$$('div.ninja').each(function(ninja){
  ninja.setStyle('visibility', 'hidden');
});
```

When you'll use it: $$ collects all the elements that match a given selector and returns them as an array of elements that also has all the `Element` methods applied that MooTools refers to as an *elements collection*. If $$ does not find any elements that match the selector, it returns an empty collection (an empty array).

By default, you can only pass tag names (`div`, `b`, `a`, etc.) to $$, but when you include `Selectors/Selectors.js`, $$ will also take richer CSS path expressions (e.g., `div.someClass a#someId`—see "Selectors" in Chapter 6).

When $$ doesn't find any matching elements for a selector, it returns an empty array.

Element Methods and Collections

When you create a collection, all the `Element` methods are applied to it; for example, `Element.setStyle` can be used with an elements collection.

```
$$('div.ninjas').setStyle('visibility', 'hidden');
//Hide all the ninjas
```

When you execute an `Element` method on an element collection, MooTools iterates over the collection and executes the method on each one. While it's possible to chain these methods, it's bad form because you would iterate over the collection twice. For example:

```
//This is bad
$$('div.ninja').setStyle('visibility',
    'hidden').addClass('invisible');

//It's the equivalent of the following
$$('div.ninjas').each(function(ninja){
    ninja.setStyle('visibility','hidden');
}).each(function(ninja){
    ninja.addClass('invisible');
});

//This is better; you only iterate once
$$('div.ninjas').each(function(ninja){
  ninja.setStyle('visibility',
    'hidden').addClass('invisible');
});
```

MooTools has numerous methods for collecting a group of elements from the DOM, but $$ is the only stand-alone function. Other methods are attached to `Element` prototypes. `Element.getElement`, `Element.getElements`, `Element.getChildren`, and others allow for element collection, too.

$E :: Element/Element.js

What it does: Returns the first element that matches the passed-in selector.

Usage:

```
//The first div in the DOM:
$E('div');
//The first link or, if no links are found,
//the first bold tag:
$E('a', 'b');
```

Example:

```
$E('div.ninja').setStyle('visibility', 'hidden');
```

When you'll use it: Much like $, it's a useful shortcut: $E is the equivalent of $$(selector)[0]. When $E does not find a match for the given selector, it returns null.

Note $E was left out of MooTools 1.2, but has been re-added for the next release. I use this method a lot, so I'm leaving this in here because it will be useful again soon. In the mean time, if you want to use this method, just add this to your own code:

```
$E = document.getElement.bind(document);
```

Element Methods for Collecting Children, Siblings, and Parents

In addition to $, $$, and $E, which allow you to collect elements from the entire document, you can use methods attached to Element by MooTools that help you select specific child elements. These work mostly like the preceding methods, except that they only select children of the element on which they are run.

`Element.getElement`: This method works just like $E; pass it a selector, and it returns the first child to match it.

```
$('myElement').getElement('div');
//Returns the first div inside myElement
```

`Element.getElements`: This method works similarly to $$; pass it a selector, and it returns a collection of children of the element that match it.

```
$('myElement').getElements('div');
//Returns the all divs inside myElement
```

`Element.getElementById`: This method works just like $; pass it an ID, and it returns the first child to match it.

```
$('myElement').getElementById('myChildElement');
//Returns the first element inside myElement
//with ID 'myChildElement'. This is the same
//as the following, which is the preferred method
$('myElement').getElement('#myChildElement');
//Note the '#'
```

`Element.getChildren`, `Element.getChild`: These methods work like `getElement` and `getElements` (you can pass these an optional selector) but are limited to direct children of the element.

`Element.getParent`, `Element.getParents`: These methods work just like `getChildren` and `getChild` (you can pass an optional selector). If you pass a selector to `getParent`, it will flow up through the DOM, inspecting each parent to find a match; otherwise, if you don't specify a selector, it returns the immediate parent of the element. `getParents` does the same but returns all the parents that match the selector (or, if no selector is specified, all the parents up to the `document` root).

`Element.getNext`, `Element.getAllNext`, `Element.getPrevious`, `Element.getAllPrevious`: These methods work like `getChild` and `getChildren`, returning the first sibling to match the selector (for `getNext`; `getPrevious` obviously gets the previous sibling), or an array of siblings for the "`All`" methods.

`Element.hasChild`: This method returns `true` if the specified element is a child (of any depth, so it can be a child of a child, for example).

```
myElement.hasChild(kid);
//Returns true if myElement contains kid
```

Setting, Getting, and Erasing Properties of Elements

The JavaScript representation of an element provides both methods and attributes. Attributes of an element can be referenced using dot or bracket notation:

```
myImg.src = "/foo.jpg";
myImg["src"] = "/foo.jpg";
```

This method of setting a property is technically deprecated. The current specification for setting an attribute is to use the `setAttribute` method, and for getting one you have `getAttribute`:

```
myImg.setAttribute('src', '/foo.jpg');
myImg.getAttribute('src'); //Returns '/foo.jpg'
```

This is a more functional approach to managing attributes, but it isn't well implemented across all the browsers. MooTools takes this and adds a lot more options and functionality, using the shorter `set` and `get` and adding into the mix the method `erase`, which lets you remove an attribute entirely.

Element.set

What it does: Sets an attribute of an element to a specified value.

Usage:

```
Element.set(property, value);
```

Example:

```
myImg.set('src', 'foo.jpg');
```

In addition to being able to get or set any attribute, you can also do things like set the innerHTML of an element:

```
myDiv.set('html', '<b>new html!</b>');
```

In native JavaScript, you'd be forced to do the following:

```
myDiv.innerHTML = '<b>new html</b>';
```

What's so bad about that? Well, in addition to not being a method (which you could delay or bind, for instance), it has cross-browser issues (attributes sometimes have different names in different browsers, and you can't use it to set every attribute as you would think you could). set and get solve these issues for you, providing a much more friendly interface to element attributes.

set has more powerful capabilities than just specifying a single attribute. For instance, you can also pass it an object of values:

```
myImg.set({
   src: '/foo.jpg',
   alt: 'this is foo',
   //Class is a reserved word in JS,
   //so we must use quotes
   'class': 'fooClass',
   //In addition to standard attributes, you can also
   //use set for some special attributes defined by
   //MooTools
   events: {
      click: function(){ alert('click!');}
   },
   styles: {
      border: '1px solid blue',
      marginTop: '10px'
   },
   etc...
});
```

When you'll use it: Any time you want to set an attribute on an element, you should use set. Note that MooTools has a few other Element methods (like setStyle) that allow you to set some specific properties. You can still use set for these if you prefer.

```
myElement.setStyle('border', '1px solid blue');
myElement.set('styles', {border: '1px solid blue'});
//Same result
```

Element.get

What it does: Allows for custom functionality, which MooTools uses to create shortcuts that are useful, but you can use them, too. MooTools adds things like get('value'), which returns the value of an input or text area.

The attributes that MooTools provides special access to are html, href, text, value, and tag, as well as shortcuts to effects (more in Chapter 9).

Usage:

```
myElement.get(property);
```

Example:

```
myInput.get('value');
myImage.get('src');
```

When you'll use it: The get method allows you to inspect an element for various attributes, and in general you should always use it to do so. As noted with set, there are some methods (like getStyle) that MooTools provides its own methods for which are the preferred methods for retrieving that information.

Element.erase

What it does: Removes an attribute value altogether.

Usage:

```
myElement.erase(property);
```

Example:

```
myImg.erase('alt');
```

When you'll use it: Sometimes (though I find somewhat rarely), you want to remove a property altogether. If you have a method that checks for an attribute on an element and performs an action based on the result, for example, then you need to remove the attribute—not just set it to some nonactive value (like an empty string).

Custom Getters and Setters and Erasers

MooTools allows you to define your own methodology for a get, set, and erase routine. This can be useful if you find you repeatedly need to process some attribute of an element. You can make a method and implement it into `Element` (see "Native.implement" in Chapter 4), or you could create your own custom getter and setter.

Say that you wanted to add a new attribute, `get/set('yellow')`. You could implement this yourself:

```
Element.Properties.yellow = {
  set: function(){
    return this.setStyle('background-color', 'yellow');
  },
  get: function(){
    return this.getStyle('background-color')=='yellow';
  },
  erase: function(){
    return this.setStyle('background-color', 'inherit');
  }
};
myDiv.set('yellow'); //It's yellow
myDiv.get('yellow'); //Returns true
```

In this way, MooTools allows you to define your own attributes and their meaning, much as it lets you extend native objects with new attributes and methods. It's a very powerful way to extend the environment to suit your needs. It's especially useful if you have a widget or effect that requires an element to work.

Element Injection and Removal

What they do: Either manipulate the content of the DOM (`inject`, `adopt`, `wraps`, `grab`, and `replaces`) or remove elements or their contents (`dispose`, `empty`, and `destroy`).

When you'll use them: Selecting and creating elements is just the tip of the iceberg with what you can do with them, but it won't do you any good if they aren't in the DOM (as they are when you create a new element—it's not part of the document until you inject it) or if they're in the wrong place.

The MooTools documentation is pretty straightforward on how to use these methods, but here's a quick rundown of them:

`Element.inject`: This method inserts or moves an element into the DOM at the specified location. The default placement is `"bottom"`, meaning that it will inject the element into the specified parent as the last child of that parent. Other options include `"before"`, `"after"`, and `"top"`.

```
myElement.inject(newParentElement);
//myElement is now the last child of newParentElement
```

```
myElement.inject(siblingElement, "before");
//myElement is now inside the same parent
//as siblingElement
//and is previous to that sibling
```

`Element.grab`: This method is just like `inject`, only in reverse—the passed-in argument is injected into the element invoking the method. The second, optional argument can be either `"top"` or `"bottom"` (the default).

```
newParentElement.grab(myElement);
//myElement is the last child of newParentElement
newParentElement.grab(myElement, "top");
//myElement is the first child of newParentElement
```

Element.adopt: This method is just like grab, except it allows multiple elements to be adopted, which are always at the bottom.

```
newParentElement.adopt(myElement, myOtherElement, etc);
```

Element.wraps: This method is just like grab, except instead of moving the target into the parent, it moves the parent to be around the target. The parent of the target becomes the parent of the element grabbing the target, and the target becomes a child of the element doing the grabbing. You can pass an optional second argument for where the child should be put into the new parent—either 'top' or 'bottom'.

```
oldParent.grab(myElement);
//oldParent now has myElement as a child
newParent.wraps(myElement, 'top'); //top is optional
//newParent is now a child of oldParent
//and myElement is now a child of newParent
```

Element.replaces: This method removes the specified element and puts a new one in its place.

```
myNewElement.replaces(myOldElement);
```

Element.empty: This method removes all the child nodes from the element using the Element.destroy method.

Element.dispose: This method removes the element from the document, but NOT from memory. This means you could inject it back into the DOM later if you wanted.

`Element.destroy`: This method removes the element from the document entirely and collects its memory. This means you CANNOT inject it back into the DOM later if you wanted. This is useful if you're managing a lot of content on a page and you need to reclaim the memory (for instance, you have an image gallery where you only want to keep 50 images in memory at a time).

Element (CSS) Classes

You can easily add and remove classes to an element and also find out whether one is already there. These are fairly self explanatory.

```
myElement.addClass('blue');
myElement.hasClass('blue'); //Returns true
myElement.removeClass('blue'); //No more blue
myElement.toggleClass('blue'); //Blue again
myElement.toggleClass('blue'); //No more blue (again)
```

Element Storage

This is perhaps one of the coolest things in MooTools, if you ask me. Simply put, element storage is the ability to store anything in JavaScript (an object, function, value, class, another element, whatever) as an attribute of an element.

You can technically do this natively like so:

```
var myFoo = new Foo();
myElement.foo = myFoo;
```

The problem with it is that it tends to leak memory when you reference certain types of objects (basically, anything except a string or a number). A lot. So it's considered very bad form—irresponsible even—to store data this way.

The excellent MooTools blog (`http://blog.mootools.net`) has this awesome explanation, and rather than rewrite it all, I'm going to just quote it because it explains it so well:

What's New in 1.2: Element Storage

http://blog.mootools.net/2008/1/22/Element_Storage

Jan. 22, 2008, Tom Occhino

When developing advanced JavaScript applications, it's sometimes beneficial to associate extra properties or attributes to DOM elements. While we have always been able to use DOM elements as storage containers for all sorts of other data, this generic technique has a few drawbacks. While the problems associated with this technique are almost exclusively Internet Explorer problems, they must be dealt with nonetheless.

Let's consider the following simple example:

```
var element = $('myElement');
element.effectInstance = new Fx.Tween(element, 'color');
element.customProperty = 'someProperty';
element.effectInstance; //The Fx.Tween instance
element.customProperty; //'someProperty'
```

As we know, IE doesn't like when objects are stored as Element attributes in this way, and the effectInstance property will leak if it's not manually managed. Another problem we've seen is that when accessing the innerHTML of any parent of our element, IE will return simple custom properties (like strings, numbers, etc.) along with the expected properties. This means that customProperty would be copied as well, which could pose a problem if it was some unique custom attribute. Obviously, of the two cases, memory management is our biggest concern here, but both are issues to consider.

A MooTools-Worthy Solution

`Element.Storage` is brand new in MooTools 1.2. It is basically an external `Hash` that stores all the custom properties and events for every element you interact with.

Let's take another look at our previous example, this time using the new `Element.Storage` API:

```
var element = $('myElement');
element.store('effectInstance',
  new Fx.Tween(element, 'color'));
element.store('customProperty', 'someProperty');
element.retrieve('effectInstance');
//The Fx.Tween instance
element.retrieve('customProperty'); //'someProperty'
```

Note that events and actions are no longer attached directly to the elements. Everything is stored in the external `Hash` and managed by MooTools, so as a developer, you have nothing to worry about. Finally, an elegant and coherent API for attaching custom properties, functions, and objects to elements.

Advanced Examples

`Element:retrieve` actually accepts an optional second parameter that will act as the default value to store if another value doesn't previously exist. It will then retrieve the value as expected.

```
$('myElement').retrieve('defaultValue',
  'Some Default Value');
//Stores and returns 'Some Default Value'
//if the key doesn't previously exist
```

Also, many users have asked about namespacing the element storage. We have responded by telling them that it already allows this since you can store objects and hashes. Consider the following example:

```
var element = $('myElement');
var data = element.retrieve('galleryData', {});
data.id = 16;
data.source = '/images/16.jpg';
data.title = 'Some Title';
//Later
$('myElement').retrieve('galleryData');
//{ id: 16, source: '/images/16.jpg',
//  title: 'Some Title' }
$('myElement').retrieve('galleryData').id; //16
```

The Elements Object

In addition to the native `Element` object, MooTools has a special type of array of elements called `Elements` (also referred to as a collection in this book). I outline the basic principal of the `Elements` object in the section "*$$* :: Element/Element.js" earlier in the chapter.

Any time you collect a group of elements from the DOM, you'll be using one of these `Elements` objects.

Elements Methods

The `Elements` object is an array of elements that has all the properties of `Array` *plus* all the methods of `Element`. So, for example, `indexOf` (an `Array` method) works:

```
$$('div').indexOf(myDiv);
```

And so does `set`, an `Element` method:

```
$$('img').set('src', '/foo.jpg');
//All the images' sources are /foo.jpg now
```

As I pointed out in the section "*$$* :: Element/Element.js," it's important to realize that this shortcut iterates over all the elements in the collection and executes the element method on each. Therefore, it's inefficient (and bad form) to chain these methods (quoting from the $$ example earlier):

```
//This is bad
$$('div.ninja').setStyle('visibility',
  'hidden').addClass('invisible');

//It's the equivalent of
$$('div.ninjas').each(function(ninja){
  ninja.setStyle('visibility','hidden');
}).each(function(ninja){
  ninja.addClass('invisible');
});

//This is better; you only iterate once
$$('div.ninjas').each(function(ninja){
  ninja.setStyle('visibility',
    'hidden').addClass('invisible');
});
```

Elements.filter

This method lets you filter the elements based on a selector (unless you don't have `Selectors.js` in your environment, in which case you can only filter on tag name):

```
var allDivs = $$('div');
    var divsWithClassBlue = allDivs.filter('.blue');
```

Other Element Methods in *Element.js*

As I stated previously, MooTools gives a lot of attention to the `Element` native. So much so that there are four separate files dedicated to the topic (outlined next). But `Element.js` alone contains numerous other methods that I haven't covered here—things like `toQueryString` and `getSelected`. These are useful in their own right, but if you understand the methods that I've covered so far, the information in the online documentation should be easy to follow.

Element.Event.js

Any time you want to make a web page interactive, you're going to have to deal with events. If the user must click something, you need to tell the browser that something should happen when they do.

Historically, this was accomplished in a few different ways. There's the inline method:

```
<a href="#" onclick="myFunction()">click me!</a>
```

The downside to this style of event management is that it's intrusive. You must describe the functionality in the same place as the data (the HTML). With the advent of things like CSS, the whole point is to present the content generically, and then style it externally. The same principal holds true for JavaScript.

Another method was to select the element out of the document and describe the event method as a property of the element:

```
document.getElementById('foo').onclick = myFunction;
```

Here the problem is that you can only ever describe one action for each event. You can't have more than one onclick, for example.

Then there's the more modern way of attaching events, which, unfortunately, is different in Internet Explorer than it is in Firefox or Safari. Here's what it looks like in Firefox:

```
document.getElementById('foo').addEventListener(
    'click', myFunction, useCapture
    //useCapture = true/false
);
```

The big problem here is that it's different in Internet Explorer, so your code must always have a conditional to do it one way for IE, and another way for everyone else. Not fun.

The other big problem with all three of these options is that they create potential for memory leaks, especially with closures (see "Closures" in the Appendix).

Adding and Removing Element Events

MooTools provides us with methods for adding events to elements that deals with the cross-browser issues and provides a more concise syntax.

Element.addEvent

What it does: Monitors an element for the specified event type (click, mouseover, etc.), and then executes the specified method, passing that method the event object that triggered it.

Usage:

```
myElement.addEvent(eventType, function);
```

Example:

```
$('myElement').addEvent('click', function(event){
  alert('you clicked me!');
});
```

When you'll use it: If you want your users to be able to interact in any way with the site, you'll need to attach event listeners to execute your code when the user does anything.

There are a few important things to note with addEvent:

- The function receives as its argument the instance of the Event class containing the event object that triggered it (see the Event native documentation in Chapter 4).

- By default, the object bound to the function (the "this") is the element to which the event was attached.

- Unlike methods such as `Array.each`, you cannot specify a third argument to set a different bound object, so you must use the more explicit `Function.bind` to change it if you need to.

Consider these examples:

```
$('myElement').addEvent('click', function(event){
  alert("your mouse is at " + event.page.x +
        " by " + event.page.y);
});

//You don't have to declare the event
//argument if you don't use it
$('myElement').addEvent('click', function(){
    this.setStyle('border', '1px solid red');
    //"this" here is $("myElement") by default
});

$('myElement').addEvent('click', function(){
    //Here we bind something else to "this"
    //in this case, a slideshow class
    this.pageForward();
}.bind(slideShowClass));
```

Element.addEvents

What it does: Allows you to attach more than one event with a single method: addEvents.

Usage:

```
myElement.addEvents(object);
```

Example:

```
myElement.addEvents({
  click: function(){ alert ('clicked!'); }
});
```

When you'll use it: If you need to attach more than one event, you can call `Element.addEvent` for each one, but you can also use `Element.addEvents` to attach several at once. The syntax is basically the same:

```
$('myElement').addEvents({
  click: function(event){
    alert("your mouse is at " + event.page.x +
          " by " + event.page.y);
  },
  mouseover: function(){
    this.setStyle('border', '1px solid red');
  },
  dblclick: function(){
    this.pageForward();
  }.bind(slideShowClass)
});
```

Element.RemoveEvent

What it does: Removes an event by passing the function you originally attached using the same syntax.

Usage:

```
myElement.removeEvent('click', function);
```

Example:

```
var foo = function(){ alert('hi there!'); };
$('myElement').addEvent('click', foo);
$('myElement').removeEvent('click', foo);
```

When you'll use it: Sometimes you need to stop monitoring an element for user interaction. For example, you might only monitor an element until the user interacts with it once. Other times, you might find that you need to ensure that there's only one event listener attached to it. If you have an event listener that alerts the user to some state when an object is clicked, you might want to remove any other click events on that element before you add another one.

You can't, however, remove an anonymous function:

```
$('myElement').addEvent('click', function(){
  alert('hi there!');
});
//This won't work!
$('myElement').removeEvent('click', function(){
  alert('hi there!');
});
```

The reason you can't do this is because each function here is a different object. Likewise, you can't remove a function that you use a method on when you attach it (like bind or pass):

```
var say = function(msg){ alert(msg); };
$('myElement').addEvent('click', say.pass('hi there!'));
$('myElement').removeEvent('click', say);
```

As outlined in "Functions" in Chapter 4, using a method on a function returns a new function with those values set to it. So say.pass('hi there!'); is not the same as say. It's a copy of say with the argument set.

To work around this, you must keep a reference to the copy:

```
var say = function(msg){ alert(msg); };
var hiThere = say.pass('hi there!');
$('myElement').addEvent('click', hiThere);
$('myElement').removeEvent('click', hiThere);
```

Element.removeEvents

What it does: Removes all of the events of a given type (e.g., all onclick events) or all the events (of any type) entirely.

Usage:

```
myElement.removeEvents([type]);
```

Example:

```
//Remove all the click events:
$('myElement').removeEvents('click');
//Remove all the events, regardless of type:
$('myElement').removeEvents();
```

When you'll use it: Sometimes you might not have the pointer to a method that was added (see the preceding examples), or you might want to make sure that the element doesn't get the same method added twice (for instance, if you add an event to alert some data, if you added the event twice, you'd alert it twice). You can remove all the events or all the events of a given type with removeEvents.

Element.fireEvent

What it does: Allows you to manually fire any events attached to an element.

Usage:

```
Element.fireEvent(type);
```

Example:

```
Element.fireEvent('click');
```

When you'll use it: Consider something like the onsubmit event for a form. Perhaps you're going to use Ajax to update some value on the server when the user submits the form, but maybe you also have some other event that might submit it, like if the user hits enter, for instance.

You'd need to first capture the enter event and then submit the form.

```
document.body.addEvent('keydown', function(event){
    if (event.key == "enter")
       $('myForm').fireEvent('submit');
});
```

This is a crude example, but it should illustrate the concept. Firing an event like this isn't something that happens often, but it does occasionally come in handy.

Element.cloneEvents

What it does: As outlined in "Creating and Cloning Elements" at the beginning of this chapter, I show how you can clone elements to create copies for various purposes, but doing so doesn't also clone the events attached to the element. You have to do that manually.

Usage:

```
myElement.cloneEvents(targetElement [, type]);
```

Example:

```
var myCopy = myElement.clone();
//Clone the click events:
myCopy.cloneEvents(myElement, 'click');
myCopy.cloneEvents(myElement); //Clone all of the events
```

Chapter 6: Utilities

MooTools contains several scripts dedicated to helping you implement code into the page you're using. I've already discussed all the native prototype extensions (on Element, Function, Array, etc.) and in the next chapter we'll cover the Class pattern for writing reusable code. In Chapter 8, I'll start reviewing some of the classes that MooTools comes with (like Fx, Drag, and Sortables).

But there's another group of scripts that kind of exist between these two groups, composed of functions and extensions that make it easier to integrate the code you write with an actual HTML document. These are the scripts in the utilities group.

Selectors

In Chapter 5, I cover the function $$, as well as numerous extensions to the Element prototype that allow you to collect elements from the DOM.

By default, these methods only allow for tag names as their arguments. When you include Selectors.js, these methods become much more powerful. This file extends their functionality to allow for any CSS selector. It doesn't change the way you'll use these methods; it only allows you to be more specific when you wish to select something from the DOM.

Here's a basic example:

```
//Without Selectors.js, all you can select
//on are tag names.
//All the divs on the page:
$$('div');
//All the divs and paragraphs
//note: this returns an array with all the divs first,
//then all the paragraphs:
$$('div', 'p');
```

```
//When you include Selectors.js, you can
//pass in CSS selectors.
//All the divs with the css class 'myClass':
$$('div.myClass')
//All the paragraphs that are inside divs:
$$('div p');
//All the bold tags in paragraphs with
//Class 'foo' in divs with class 'myClass':
$$('div.myClass p.foo b');
```

This functionality is applied to any of the methods that accept a selector as their argument. So in addition to $$, the same is true for the following element methods:

Element.getElement	Element.getAllNext
Element.getElements	Element.getFirst
Element.match	Element.getLast
Element.getPrevious	Element.getParent
Element.getAllPrevious	Element.getParents
Element.getNext	Element.getChildren

Complex CSS3 Expressions

In addition to standard CSS expressions, as in the examples in the previous section, Selectors.js also allows you to select on element properties such as name, value, or href using standard CSS3 expressions (see http://www.w3.org/TR/css3-selectors/#attribute-representation).

Example:

```
//All the mail-to links on the page:
$$('a[href^=mailto:]');
```

The following expressions are supported:

=	The property is equal to the value.
^=	The property begins with the value.
$=	The property ends with the value.
!=	The property is not equal to the value.
*=	The property contains the value.
~=	The property is found when the value is split on spaces (so ~=foo matches "blah foo bar" but not "blahfoobar").
|=	The property is found when the value is split on dashes (so |=foo matches "blah-foo-bar" but not "blahfoobar").

Here are a few more examples:

```
//All the inputs where name equals 'email'
$$('input[name=email]')
//All the images with urls that end in .gif:
$$('img[src$=gif]')
//All the links without target="_blank":
$$('a[target!=_blank]')
```

Note that these expressions can take double or single quotes when you want to search for something that has a space or other character:

```
$$('input[name!="user[username]"]')
$$('img[src$=".gif"]')
```

Using Structural Expressions

In addition to the attribute expressions in the previous section, MooTools also supports structural selectors (see http://www.w3.org/TR/css3-selectors/#structural-pseudos). These let you select elements based on their order in the document—every third paragraph, for example. You can also do searches for all the enabled form elements, or all the empty ones.

Here are the structural selectors that MooTools supports:

:enabled	The element is not disabled.
:disabled	The element is disabled.
:empty	The element has no children.
:contains(text)	The element's inner HTML contains the value.
:nth-child(expression)	This returns every child that matches the expression (see examples that follow).
:even	This returns every other (even) child.
:odd	This returns every other (odd) child.
:first	The element is the first child.
:last	The element is the last child.
:only	The element is the only child of its parent.

Examples:

```
//All the paragraphs that are the first child
//of their parents:
$$('p:first');
//Every other link inside paragraphs:
$$('p a:even');
//Every 3rd list item in a specific list:
$$('ul#myList li:nth-child(3n)');
//All the links in paragraphs where the link is
//the last child:
$$('p a:last');
```

See the online documentation for MooTools for more details, as well as the documentation for CSS3 selectors.

DomReady

In the Appendix, which covers core concepts in JavaScript, one of the topics I discuss is DomReady.

MooTools implements a custom event for DomReady, and you'll use it on nearly every page that includes your JavaScript.

The DomReady Custom Event

What it does: Runs any JavaScript that should wait for the document to load.

Usage:

```
window.addEvent('domready', function);
```

Example:

```
window.addEvent('domready', function(){
  $$('div.error').each(function(div){
    div.setStyle('border', '1px solid #F00');
  });
});
```

When you'll use it: As outlined in the Appendix, the native event that was historically used was the onload event. This event, however, waits until all the assets on the page (e.g., images) have loaded before it fires. If you have code that is meant to run as soon as the document is ready, the earliest moment you could run it is when the HTML is delivered, but not necessarily after all the images load. MooTools provides a custom event (determined by various means for different browsers) for this HTML-is-ready moment.

Any code that you author that references the DOM (either by collecting elements, injecting new ones, or altering existing ones) should wait for this DomReady event.

JSON

JSON is a lightweight data-interchange format based on the object notation in JavaScript. It is a text format that is completely language independent but uses conventions that are familiar to programmers of the C family of languages. Think of it as XML for JavaScript.

Declaring a native object in JavaScript looks like this (note that you can use single or double quotes; it doesn't matter):

```
{fruits: ['apple', 'pear'], veggies: ['peas', 'beans']}
```

In JSON, the same data would look like this:

```
{"fruits":["apple","pear"],"veggies":["peas","beans"]}
```

They're the same for all intents and purposes. The important thing is that the JSON standard is something that the JavaScript parser can understand.

Consequently, using JSON as a method to transmit data between the client and the server is much easier than using XML. Visit http://www.json.org for more information as well as plug-ins for nearly every programming environment to convert XML to JSON and back again.

MooTools and JSON

MooTools contains methods useful for converting objects to and from JSON. These methods are fairly straightforward.

JSON.encode

What it does: Converts any object or array into a JSON string.

Usage:

```
JSON.encode(myObj);
```

Example:

```
JSON.encode({
    fruits: ['apple', 'pear'],
    veggies: ['peas', 'beans']
});
//Returns
'{"fruits":["apple","pear"],"veggies":["peas","beans"]}'
```

When you'll use it: Mostly you'll use JSON with Ajax to transmit and receive data from a server. It's also possible that you'll use it to store data elsewhere (like in a cookie), but mostly it's used to communicate with other computers.

JSON.decode

What it does: Allows you to take a JSON string and convert it back into a native JavaScript object. This is the reciprocal method of JSON.encode.

Usage:

```
JSON.decode(jsonString[, secure]);
```

Example:

```
JSON.decode('{"fruits":["apple","pear"],
            "veggies":["peas","beans"]}');
```

When you'll use it: As with JSON.encode, this method is likely to be used when you're communicating with a server. You'll use it to decode the response.

Note that, since JSON data is evaluated by the browser, it represents a security threat. If the JSON you decode turns out to be malicious code, it will be run. Consequently, you should ensure that the JSON is either coming from a secure source (e.g., the same domain as the document) or you should use the `secure` argument to ensure that the string being evaluated is an object and not a function.

```
Json.decode("alert('you just got haxored!')", true);
//Returns null
```

Cookie

Let's face it, the interface to manage cookies in native JavaScript is a pain, which is why if you audit the JavaScript of nearly any web site that uses cookies, you'll find functions to do it for you.

MooTools, of course, gives us its own helpful methods for managing cookies.

Cookie.write

What it does: Allows you to write a cookie value to the client specifying only the options you need.

Usage:

```
Cookie.write(key, value[, options]);
```

Example:

```
//Simple session cookie
Cookie.write('username', 'fred');
Cookie.write('font-preference', 'large', {
  //Make this cookie available to the entire site:
  path: '/',
  //for 30 days:
  duration: 30,
  //Make it available to subdomains:
  domain: 'mysite.com',
  //Only readable if the user is accessing via https:
  secure: true
});
```

When you'll use it: You'll use this method whenever you want to store stateful information for the user.

Cookie.read

What it does: Returns the value of a cookie from the client (always a `string`) or else returns `false` if no value was found.

Usage:

```
Cookie.read(name);
```

Example:

```
var preference = Cookie.read('font-preference');
```

When you'll use it: You'll use this method whenever you need to retrieve the value of a cookie.

Cookie.dispose

What it does: Removes a cookie from the client.

Usage:

```
Cookie.dispose(name);
```

Example:

```
Cookie.dispose('username');
```

When you'll use it: You'll use this method whenever you want to completely remove a cookie from the client.

Swiff

Adding Flash content to a page is not especially difficult, but there are some cross-browser issues with how one does it. Additionally, interacting with that Flash element with JavaScript takes a bit of labor, and consequently MooTools provides methods to manage this for you.

Swiff Constructor

What it does: Creates and returns a Flash object with the supplied parameters.

Usage:

```
new Swiff(path[, options]);
```

Example:

```
var mySwiff = new Swiff('/flash-movie.swf', {
  id: 'myBeautifulMovie'
  width: 500,
  height: 400,
  params: {
    wmode: 'opaque',
    bgcolor: '#ff3300'
  },
  vars: {
    myVariable: myJsVar,
    myVariableString: 'hello'
  },
  container: $('someElement')
});
```

Note that when creating the instance of swiff, if you do not specify a value for the container option, it does not inject the Flash element into the document. You'll still need to do that yourself (see "Swiff.replaces, Swiff.inject").

When you'll use it: You'll use this method whenever you need to embed Flash into your pages. It eliminates cross-browser issues and simplifies the interface for creating these elements.

Swiff.replaces, Swiff.inject

What they do: Allow you to inject a Flash object into a document.

Usage:

```
mySwiff.inject(element[, where]);
  //See Element.inject for details
mySwiff.replaces(element);
  //See Element.replaces for details
```

Examples:

```
mySwiff.inject('myElement', 'after');
mySwiff.replaces('myElement');
```

When you'll use them: When you use the constructor for Swiff (i.e., new Swiff), it creates the element but doesn't inject it into the document unless you specify a value for the container option. You'll use these methods to put them into the page.

Swiff.remote

What it does: Calls an ActionScript method from JavaScript.

Usage:

```
mySwiff.remote(function);
```

Example:

```
var obj = new Swiff('myMovie.swf');
obj.remote('myFlashFunctionToExecute');
```

When you'll use it: This method is useful for running methods in your Flash file when something happens in the browser and you want to send information to the Flash environment. Note that your Flash file must be compiled with the ExternalInterface component. (See the Adobe documentation on ExternalInterface for more information.)

Chapter 7: Classes and Inheritance

MooTools includes mechanisms for tapping into JavaScript's native inheritance model (See also "Prototypal Inheritance" in the Appendix). The syntax looks very similar to the kinds of object-oriented models found in Java and even uses the name "Class" in the context. Still, it's important to understand that the model here is still JavaScript's.

MooTools classes implement functionality into objects that can be initialized into numerous stateful instances. Each instance is an object with methods and properties unique to itself but based on the methods and properties in the class. Creating an instance of, say, Widget and assigning it specific values (options like location, visibility, etc.) returns that instance. You can then create another instance of Widget with different options and execute methods on either of them without affecting the other.

In my experience, there are two types of code in JavaScript: reusable code and implementation code. The former includes all the things that you might ever want to use again—date pickers, form validators, sortable tables, whatever. The latter is the code you write on a specific page to tell it that these things are present and configured for the current content. All your implementation code should be a set of namespaced functions (myPage.load, myPage.search, etc.), and everything else—the reusable code—should be classes (FormValidator, DatePicker, Gallery). In this way, every page sets up new instances of these classes, passing along the data and configurations for them that are unique to the given environment.

Using the Class Constructor

What it does: The Class constructor creates functionality for defining reusable Class objects that can be extended and inherited from.

Usage:

```
new Class(properties);
```

Example:

```
var SimpleClass = new Class({
  initialize: function(options){
    this.options = options;
  },
  someProperty: 'foo',
  someMethod: function(msg){ alert(msg); }
});
```

When you'll use it: MooTools contains a very elegant structure for authoring functionality that can be extended and altered in different contexts. JavaScript itself has the core capacity for this functionality, but no native methods to make use of it. Historically, people either didn't make use of it or had to author their own methods to be able to make use of the inheritance model in JavaScript.

Making best use of JavaScript's prototypal inheritance model requires that you understand that model well. It's important that you grasp how JavaScript's constructor model works (see "'this' and Binding" in the Appendix) and how JavaScript's prototypal inheritance model works (see "Prototypal Inheritance" also in the Appendix).

Binding and prototypal inheritance are the two concepts at the heart of MooTools, and very little functionality in the library avoids using them.

The core functionality for managing inheritance is the `Class` function. Remember that by convention, any function that begins with an uppercase letter requires the use of the `new` constructor when using it. So every class that you author should begin with an uppercase letter so that you know it needs `new` to initialize it.

The `properties` argument is an object of name/value properties for the class that defines what each instance should have when it is initialized. Say you have the following very simple class:

```
var Human = new Class({
  isAlive: true,
  energy: 1,
  eat: function(){
    this.energy++;
  }
});
```

You've now defined some very simple functionality for your `Human` class. Whenever you want a new instance of `Human`, you just call it with the `new` constructor:

```
var bob = new Human();
```

This instance—bob—is an instance of `Human`, and it has the properties `isAlive`, `energy`, and `eat`. These properties have the default values defined in your `Human` class, but you can change them easily enough.

```
bob.eat(); //bob.energy is now 2
```

Initialization

When classes are invoked with their constructor, all the properties in the object passed in are applied to the new class and are available to each instance (like with `Human.eat` earlier). MooTools looks for a special property called `initialize` that it will execute whenever a new instance is created.

Here's what that might look like:

```
var Human = new Class({
   initialize: function(name, age){
      this.name = name;
      this.age = age;
   },
   isAlive: true,
   energy: 1,
   eat: function(){
      this.energy++;
   }
});
var bob = new Human('Bob', 20);
//bob.age = 20
//bob.name = 'Bob'
```

Here you have a class with default properties and methods (like `isAlive` and `eat`), but not all `Humans` are necessarily the same, so you allow arguments to be passed to the constructor, which are passed to the `initialize` method at invocation.

Classes aren't required to have an `initialize` method. If you have a class that doesn't do anything when you initialize it, you can omit this method. Classes that are meant to be implemented by other classes (see "Implementing Classes into Other Classes" later in this chapter) usually don't have an `initialize` method because they would overwrite the method in the class that you blend them into. Otherwise, you'll use this method to set up the state of the class when the user creates it. Often options and arguments are passed in, and the `initialize` method stores those in the instance of the class and maybe processes them.

Inheritance

Creating classes is a really powerful way to reuse functionality. You can define all the methods and default values for a widget or UI component and then create new instances of those things over and over again. If you discover a bug in your code, you only have to fix it in one place. It's object-oriented programming in JavaScript, which for a long time was a concept that just didn't seem to be in the language.

But even this basic ability is somewhat limited if you can't extend that functionality when you need to. If you have a class that validates form inputs, that's awesome, but what if you need to make a class that does so a little differently? Copying all that code into another class doesn't make sense, and thankfully you don't have to.

MooTools offers two ways to get more out of the classes that you write with Extends and Implements—two special properties of classes that let you get more mileage out of the code you write.

Implement vs. Extend

The Extends property is used to employ another class as a blueprint for the one you are creating, while the Implements property is used to enumerate other classes whose methods should be added to the one you are creating.

In addition to these two properties are two methods for extending and implementing classes: Class.extend and Class.implement. Class.extend is used to add properties directly to a class, while Class.implement modifies the prototype of the class.

These distinctions are further explained next, as it's important that you learn when to use each if you want to get the full power of MooTools.

Extending Classes

Classes have a special property called Extends that allows you to build upon another class very easily. As stated earlier, Extends specifies an object (a Class) that will act as the template for the new class you define. Let's build on the Human class shown earlier and make a Ninja class.

```
var Human = new Class({
  initialize: function(name, age){
    this.name = name;
    this.age = age;
  },
  isAlive: true,
  energy: 1,
  eat: function(){
    this.energy++;
  }
});
var Ninja = new Class({
  Extends: Human,
  initialize: function(side, name, age){
    this.side = side;
    this.parent(name, age);
  },
  energy: 100,
  attack: function(target){
    this.energy = this.energy - 5;
    target.isAlive = false;
  }
});
var bob = new Human('Bob', 25);
var blackNinja =
  new Ninja('evil', 'Nin Tendo', 'unknown');
//blackNinja.isAlive = true
//blackNinja.name = 'Nin Tendo'
blackNinja.attack(bob);
//bob never had a chance
```

Here you have your Human class and another class that builds upon it. If you inspect properties in blackNinja, you find properties from the Ninja class and the Human class.

Let's consider the two properties in Ninja that overlap those in Human: energy and initialize. In the Human class, you've defined the default for `energy` as `1`, but ninjas get `100`. This will override the value for `energy` defined in `Human`.

Then there's the `initialize` method. Both classes have one, and here you see a special property for methods: `this.parent`. Classes that extend other classes can have overlapping methods but retain the ability to execute the method that they overwrite. In this way, you can extend a method in a class, with logic executed before and/or after the parent method is called.

`Extends` is quite powerful, allowing you to overwrite methods in the parent class and optionally execute that overwritten method. Note that you must still pass the arguments to the parent method that it expects to receive, even if the new method you've defined takes different arguments. By using `Extends`, you can create small classes that do one thing well and then build upon them with more specific functionality. The result is more reusable code.

Extending Classes into Themselves

Extending a class into itself allows you to alter the way its instances behave without creating a new name for the result. You essentially get to add more stuff to the class itself. Why do this? Say you want to alter a class in a particular environment without changing it everywhere.

Here's an example of what this would look like:

```
//Continuing from the Human and Ninja classes earlier
Ninja = new Class({
    Extends: Ninja,
    kills: 0,
    attack: function(target){
      this.parent(target);
      this.kills++;
    }
});
```

Here you add functionality to the `Ninja` class—now you can keep track of how many targets each `Ninja` has offed (I know, it's a bit morbid, but hey, that's just how ninjas are—it's *what they do*). But you can see the advantage; you can still call the parent method as defined in what *used* to be `Ninja.attack`, so you don't have to rewrite that logic. You can add your own additional logic that happens before or after you call the parent function.

The only downside to this method is that any instances of `Ninja` that have already been created (as well as any classes that have already been created by extending this one) will not have this functionality, so it's important that you have this kind of extension defined before you create any instances of the class or extend it further.

Implementing Classes

Extending classes allows you to create new classes based on the templates of old ones, making use of the properties defined in the parent classes, adding new properties, and overwriting ones that you wish to alter. But what if you want to change how an existing class works? That's where implementing classes comes into play.

Implementing functionality into classes has one big positive and one big negative. On the positive side, when you implement functionality into a class, all instances of the class are affected immediately (unlike using `Extends` to extend a class back onto itself, as discussed in the preceding section). On the negative side, you don't have access to what used to be defined for methods—there's no `this.parent`. You must overwrite the entire property when you implement changes. This is because `implement` changes the prototype of the object you are modifying, essentially altering the parent instead of the object itself.

There are two ways to implement functionality into a `Class`. The first is to use a method that comes with every class called `implement`. Here's what it looks like:

```
//Continuing from our Human and Ninja classes earlier
Ninja.implement({
   kills: 0,
   attack: function(target){
     target.isAlive = false;
     this.energy = this.energy - 5;
     this.kills++;
   }
});
```

Unlike with the example in the "Extending Classes into Themselves" section, you can't reference `this.parent`, so you must reauthor all of the functionality in the `attack` method. This can be a real pain, which is why extending classes into themselves is so useful.

`Implements` is really meant to be used to combine classes, and consequently there is no notion of a parent. If you add all the methods of class A into class B, class B now has the methods of class A in its prototype, but there is no "parent" relationship between class A and class B, which brings us to the next section.

Implementing Classes into Other Classes

It's much more likely that you'll use implementing to add functionality from one class to another via the `Implements` property. By implementing functionality from class into another, you can identify patterns that are shared across numerous classes and push that functionality into all of them. This creates an enormous opportunity to not only deliver less code to the browser, but also reuse what you write.

Consider this example:

```
var Warrior = new Class({
  energy: 100,
  kills: 0,
  attack: function(target){
    target.isAlive;
    this.energy = this.energy - 5;
    this.kills++;
  }
});
var Human = new Class({
  initialize: function(name, age){
    this.name = name;
    this.age = age;
  },
  isAlive: true,
  energy: 1,
  eat: function(){
    this.energy++;
  }
});
var Ninja = new Class({
  Extends: Human,
  Implements: [Warrior],
  initialize: function(side, name, age){
    this.side = side;
    this.parent(name, age);
  }
});
var Samurai = new Class({
  Extends: Human,
  Implements: [Warrior],
  side: 'good'
});
```

This set of examples extends the Human class into both the Ninja and Samurai classes, making use of that functionality twice. The methods contained in Warrior are also implemented into both these classes, but the difference here is that the `Warrior` methods and properties don't overlap with anything in the `Human` class.

`Implements` is mostly used with helper classes—collections of commonly used functionality that often gets employed in numerous classes. Examples of these include the `Options` class and the `Events` class.

The idea here is to project small bits of reusable functionality into your classes. If you write things well, you end up with all these little LEGO-like blocks that can be snapped together to get robust functionality, while each individual class does one thing specifically.

The best way to understand the potential of MooTools' class architecture is to look inside MooTools itself. The library is comprised of lots of these little blocks, and it extends and grows on itself to provide robust functionality, while each piece is as simple as it can be.

Chapter 8: Getting Started with Classes

Chapter 7 covers the basics of writing classes. These reusable chunks of code are the building blocks of your application. MooTools itself offers numerous classes for you to use to create effects, drag functionality, tooltips, and more.

In this chapter, I'll cover some of the basics of using these classes. The conventions outlined here are true of nearly all the classes that come with MooTools and will likely be true of most of the classes you write for your own use.

Class.Extras

Because two of the goals of MooTools is to make it easy to reuse code and to eliminate duplication of effort, several patterns get used over and over again in MooTools.

Three commonly used patterns in MooTools classes are options, events, and chaining. `Class.Extras.js` contains three classes that are designed to be implemented into other classes; they aren't very useful on their own, but implemented into another class, they make that class much more useful.

The Options Class

What it does: This class is designed to be implemented into other classes. The options convention allows users to pass in none, some, or all of the optional values for a class, overwriting only the default values that they need to. By defining default behaviors in your class, you can make the interface both highly flexible and easier to use.

When you look at the documentation for a MooTools class, you'll see these defined as a list of named arguments that can be passed in (or not) along with their default values.

These options passed in are then passed to the setOptions method defined in the Options class. Because you are implementing the Options class into your class, this method is now part of your class, too.

Usage:

```
new Class({
   Implements: Options,
   options: { /*default options*/ },
   initialize: function(arg1, arg2, arg3, options){
      this.setOptions(options);
   }
});
```

Example:

```
var Widget = new Class({
   Implements: Options,
   options: {
      color: '#fff',
      size: {
         width: 100,
         height: 100
      }
   },
   initialize: function(options){
      this.setOptions(options);
   }
});
var myWidget = new Widget({
   color: '#f00',
   size: {
      width: 200
   }
});

//myWidget.options is now:
//{color: #f00, size: {width: 200, height: 100}}
```

When you'll use it: The options convention blends together the default values (using `$merge`). This allows you to define a default state for your class that users can easily override, but doesn't force them to specify all the possible values. The result is a very flexible class with as many options as you care to implement without overloading the interface to the class. It also has two other nice consequences: 1) you don't end up with classes that require a dozen arguments, and 2) if you change the options in the class at a later date, you don't have to go find all the places that reference the class to create a compatibility layer to accomodate old code that still uses the old options.

Note   In general, you should consider the `options` object read-only in your code. You can (and should) reference `this.options` in your code to read the state that the user has defined, but you should *not* alter it directly. Instead you should use `setOptions` to alter it.

```
. . .
this.setStyle('color', this.options.color); //Yes
this.options.color = '#000000'; //No
this.setOptions({color: '#000000'}); //Yes
```

The Events Class

Another often-used pattern for classes are events. These work just like the events on elements (like `onclick`), and the interface is the same. Using `Events` in your classes allows flexibility where the class might do something in response to some other action. The events you define provide hooks into these actions. Consider a slideshow, for example. You might have events for when the user clicks forward or backward and events for when the user reaches the end of the slideshow (or back up to the start).

Because your class handles all these behaviors, the appropriate place to put the logic to determine that these actions occur are in your class. Later, when you implement an instance of the class into your page, you might need to add additional functionality that should run when these events occur.

addEvent, addEvents, fireEvent, removeEvent, removeEvents

What they do: These methods work much like their countparts on the `Element` prototype, allowing you to attach functions to specific events.

Usage:

```
new Class({
   Implements: Events,
   complete: function(){
     this.fireEvent('complete');
   }
});
```

Example:

```
var Widget = new Class({
   Implements: Events,
   initialize: function(element){
     ...
   },
   complete: function(){
     this.fireEvent('complete'[, arguments]);
   }
});

var myWidget = new Widget();
myWidget.addEvent('complete', myFunction);
```

When you'll use them: Unlike `Element`, there is no concept of a "native" event (like `onclick` or `onmouseover`) for a class. The events on a class are whatever you choose to call them. In order for them to be useful, you must include in your class calls to `fireEvent` for them to be executed. By adding events to your class, you make it much more useful in different contexts.

Events and Options

When you implement both Options and Events into your class, a bit of special magic occurs. When users initialize the class and pass in options, they can pass in event options as well. These will automatically get passed to addEvent when you pass the options to setOptions.

Example:

```
var Widget = new Class({
  Implements: [Events, Options],
  initialize: function(element, options){
    this.element = $(element);
    this.setOptions(options);
  },
  complete: function(){
    this.fireEvent('complete', this.element);
  }
});
var myWidget = new Widget($('myElement'), {
  onComplete: myFunction
});
```

Here the user has passed in as one of the options a function for onComplete. When you pass the options to setOptions, any option that begins with "on" that is a function will be passed to addEvent automatically for the complete event.

Note   Any options that begin with "on" that are functions will be removed from the options when you pass the options to setOptions. This means that if the user passes in a function for onComplete, in the options, this.options.onComplete won't be defined, as it's removed in the process.

Note   You can actually reference either the event with "on" or without it. If you use fireEvent or addEvent and reference onComplete or complete, you'll get the same result. By convention, MooTools drops the "on" for both element events and class events for consistency, but if you use the "on" with classes, it's smart enough to know which one you're referring to.

The Chain Class

MooTools also contains functionality similar to Events that lets you build a chain of functions to execute one after the other. Think of this as "when you're finished, do this next thing" functionality.

Chain.chain

What it does: The chain method pushes a function onto a stack of methods defining the order of things to do next. When the method is executed, it is removed from the stack.

Usage:

```
var Widget = new Class({ Implements: Chain });
Widget.chain(function);
```

Example:

```
var Widget = new Class({
    Implements: Chain,
    someMethod: function(){
        //Some code that does stuff
        this.callChain();
    }
});
Widget.chain(function(){ alert('this comes next!'); });
Widget.someMethod();
//Alerts the message when someMethod finishes
```

When you'll use it: This method gets used mostly in the Fx class. Typically, it's used when a class does something immediately and then completes, and often the class also has an onComplete event that is fired at the same time.

The difference between adding a method to a chain and adding it as an event is that when you add it as an event, it will get fired every time the event is fired (until you remove it), while a chained function will only get called once. Here's an example of it working on its own (which isn't that useful):

```
var myChain = new Chain();
myChain.chain(
    function(){ alert('do dishes'); },
    function(){ alert('put away clean dishes'); }
);
myChain.callChain(); //Will alert 'do dishes'.
myChain.callChain(); //Will alert 'put away clean
                     // dishes'.
```

And here's a more useful example using `Fx.Tween`:

```
var myTween = new Fx.Tween(myElement);
myTween.start('opacity', 0).chain(function(){
  myTween.start('opacity', 1);
});
```

Chain.callChain

What it does: This calls the next method on the chain stack, passing any arguments passed to it (they are optional).

Usage:

```
myChain.callChain(arguments);
```

Example:

See the example in "Chain.chain" earlier.

When you'll use it: In order for the `Chain` class to really work, you have to call the next method on the stack whenever the operation that's being performed is complete. Consider an effect—let's say you're fading the element in using its CSS opacity property. Over the duration of the effect, you repeatedly increment the value of the opacity until it reaches 1, and then you stop. At this point, you must execute `this.callChain` to call the next method on the chain stack.

Chain.clearChain

What it does: This removes all methods from the chain stack.

Usage:

```
myWidget.clearChain();
```

When you'll use it: Sometimes it's necessary to clear the chain to stop a behavior from continuing. This is especially true if you add things to the chain from within the class itself (which in general I don't recommend).

Chapter 9: Fx

Now comes the fun part of MooTools—the effects. Everything I've covered up to this point has been about the utility of writing JavaScript with MooTools and how to do so efficiently and without duplicating code. But the effects are where MooTools really shines.

Fx and Fx.CSS

The `Fx` class is one you'll likely not use directly. It's a foundation layer for all the other effect extensions. You're more likely to use the extensions than you are these two core files, so I'm not going to spend a lot of time on them. It's conceivable that you might extend one or the other to write your own effect, but even that is doubtful; if you were to undertake writing an effect, it's more likely you'd extend `Fx.Tween`, `Fx.Morph`, or `Fx.Elements` (which MooTools considers a plug-in).

What is interesting and useful to learn about the `Fx` class are the options and methods it defines, as all the other effects extend these and add to them.

Fx Options

Every effect extension accepts the following options in addition to any arguments and options that are defined by the extension. This is straight from the MooTools documentation:

- `fps`: (*Number*: defaults to 50) The frames per second for the transition.

- `unit`: (*String*: defaults to `false`) The unit, for example, "px", "em", or "%". See `Element.setStyle` in Chapter 5.

- `link`: (*String*: defaults to "ignore") Can be "ignore", "cancel", or "link".

  - **"ignore"**: Any calls made to start while the effect is running will be ignored.

- **"cancel"**: Any calls made to start while the effect is running will take precedence over the currently running transition. The new transition will start immediately, canceling the one that is currently running.

- **"chain"**: Any calls made to start while the effect is running will be chained up and will take place as soon as the current effect has finished, one after another.

- `duration`: (*Number*: defaults to 500) The duration of the effect in milliseconds. Can also be one of the following:

  - **"short"**: 250 ms

  - **"normal"**: 500 ms

  - **"long"**: 1000 ms

- `transition`: (*Function*: defaults to `Fx.Transitions.Sine.easeInOut`) The equation to use for the effect; see "Fx.Transitions" later in this chapter. Also accepts a string in the following form:

  - `transition[:in][:out]`: For example, "linear", "quad:in", "back:in", "bounce:out", "elastic:out", "sine:in:out".

Fx Events

Much like the preceding options, all effect extensions have these events (though they may have more):

- `onStart`: The function to execute when the effect begins.

- `onCancel`: The function to execute when you manually stop the effect.

- `onComplete`: The function to execute after the effect has processed.

- `onChainComplete`: The function to execute when using `link 'chain'` (see options earlier). It gets called after all effects in the chain have completed.

Fx.start

What it does: All the effect extensions have a `start` method that starts the effect, which will continue until the transition is complete or the effect is canceled.

Because each extension changes different things (`Fx.Tween` changes a single style property, `Fx.Morph` will change many, and `Fx.Elements` will change numerous style properties across numerous elements), the argument passed to start differs from extension to extension.

When `start` is called, it fires the `onStart` event and begins the transition. If only one parameter of a transition is defined, the CSS property will be transitioned from its current state to the one defined.

Usage:

```
myEffect.start(arguments);
```

Example:

```
new Fx.Tween($('myElement')).start('opacity', 1);
```

When you'll use it: This method will transition the opacity of the element from its current state (if no starting state is specified) to the state specified. If the element is already at that state, no transition will occur (though the `onComplete` event will still be called and the `chain` will still be called—see "The Chain Class" in Chapter 8).

Here we specify the starting state:

```
new Fx.Tween($('myElement')).start('opacity', 0, 1);
```

This will transition the opacity from zero to one, regardless of the current state.

Fx.set

What it does: The set method works just like the start method, except no transition is applied (and neither the onComplete method nor the chain is called).

Usage:

```
myEffect.set(arguments);
```

Example:

```
new Fx.Tween($('myElement')).set('opacity', 1);
//Opacity is immediately set to 1
```

When you'll use it: The set method is useful to quickly reset the state of a CSS property. For Fx.Tween, it's not much different from Element.setStyle, but for something like Fx.Scroll or Fx.Elements, set is a bit more useful in allowing you to change the state of the effect.

Fx.cancel, Fx.pause, Fx.resume

What they do: These methods let you stop an effect entirely (Fx.cancel) or pause it and resume it later (Fx.pause, Fx.resume). Fx.cancel will fire the onCancel event (but does not call the chain method; instead it clears the chain with clearChain).

Usage:

```
myEffect.pause(); //Pauses the effect
myEffect.resume(); //Resumes a paused effect
myEffect.cancel(); //Cancels a running effect entirely
```

When you'll use them: It's actually somewhat rare that I find myself using these methods, but there are occasions where user interaction might cause you to pause or cancel an effect. Note that when you pause or cancel an effect, the CSS property that was being transitioned will be left in whatever state it was in when you stopped the effect. So if you're fading something in and then stop the transition halfway through, the element will still be in that halfway state. You can use `Fx.set` in a case like this to set the state to whatever you want.

Fx.Tween

What it does: The simplest effect you'll likely use is `Fx.Tween`. This class transitions a single CSS property from one state to another. It's deceptively easy to use. When used properly, you can use it to create a highly engaging and expressive user experience.

Usage:

```
new Fx.Tween(element[, options]);
```

Example:

```
var myEffect = new Fx.Tween($('myElement'), {
  property: 'width',
  duration: 500, //Transition over half a second
});
//Transition from 0px wide to 100px wide:
myEffect.start(0, 100);
//Transition from the current width to 200px:
myEffect.start(200);
//You can also specify the property in the
//start method instead of the options
var myEffect = new Fx.Tween($('myElement'));
//Transition opacity to 1:
myEffect.start('opacity', 1);
//Transition width from zero to 100:
myEffect.start('width', 0, 100);
```

When you'll use it: `Fx.Tween` is the most basic effect in MooTools. When you need to fade something in or move it to a new location or change its size or color, `Fx.Tween` is all you need.

Element.tween

What it does: Many of the effects extensions also extend the `Element` prototype to provide shortcuts to start an effect.

Usage:

```
myElement.tween(property, startvalue[, endvalue]);
//If endvalue isn't set, startvalue will be used for
//the end value, and the start value will be the
//current value
```

Example:

```
//Transition opacity to 1:
$('myElement').tween('opacity', 1);
//Transition width from 0 to 100:
$('myElement').tween('width', 0, 100);
```

When you'll use it: This shortcut method not only saves you a few keystrokes, but also makes your code a little easier to read. I use it almost all the time that I want to tween an element, so maybe the title here should be "When you won't use it." The reason not to use it is when you need to have more than one effect to use for different properties. Maybe you have one transition that you use for showing an element (with different transitions, durations, etc.) than the one for hiding it. You could change these values before using the shortcut again, or you could have two instances of the effect.

Using Element.get/set with Fx.tween

What they do: The shortcut is managed using element storage (see Chapter 5). When you first use the shortcut, a new instance of `Fx.Tween` is created and stored for the element as "tween." Subsequent calls to this shortcut just reuse this instance. This means you can modify the properties of this "built-in" version of `Fx.Tween` by using `Element.get` and `Element.set` (see Chapter 5).

Usage:

```
//Set the options for the "built-in"
//instance of Fx.Tween:
myElement.set('tween', options);
//Retrieve the "built-in" instance of Fx.Tween:
myElement.get('tween');
```

Examples:

```
//Cancels a running effect:
myElement.get('tween').cancel();
myElement.set('tween', {
  //Change the duration for the "built-in" instance:
  duration: 1000
});
```

When you'll use them: These two methods are useful in managing the instance of Fx.Tween that gets created when you use the .tween shortcut. Setting the options for the duration or transition, for example, gives you greater control over what the effect looks like. Just be aware that there's only one of these built-in instances. If you need more than one instance, you'll need to use the constructor (new Fx.Tween).

Fx.Morph

What it does: This class is very similar to Fx.Tween in most respects except that it allows you to transition more than one property at the same time.

Usage:

```
var myEffect = new Fx.Morph(element[, options]);
myEffect.start(to);
```

Example:

```
var myEffect = new Fx.Morph($('myElement'), {
  duration: 1000
});
myEffect.start({
  width: 100, //Transition the width to 100
  height: [0, 100], //Transition height from 0 to 100
  opacity: 1 //Transition opacity to 1
});
```

When you'll use it: You can use `Fx.Morph` to achieve the same results as `Fx.Tween` (specifying only one property to transition), but really this class is useful when you're transitioning several attributes at once.

Element.morph

What it does: Just like `Element.tween`, `Element.morph` is a shortcut to a "built-in" instance of `Fx.Morph`.

Usage:

```
myElement.morph(to);
```

Example:

```
$('myElement').morph({ width: 100, height: 100});
```

When you'll use it: As outlined with `Element.tween`, this shortcut to the "built-in" instance of `Fx.Morph` is what I use most of the time. The times when you won't use it are the same with `Fx.Tween`/`Element.tween`, so I'll direct you to the earlier section where I go into those details.

Element.set/get with Fx.Morph

You can use `Element.set` and `Element.get` to access the "built-in" instance of `Fx.Morph` just as with `Fx.Tween`. I won't illustrate that here, but read the earlier section on how its done with `Fx.Tween` and refer to the MooTools documentation for more.

Using CSS Selectors with Fx.Morph

What it does: One of `Fx.Morph`'s neat tricks is the ability for you to pass it a CSS selector instead of an object with properties to change. Think of this as analogous to `Element.addClass`, where you add a CSS class and this changes the style of the element, except here it does so with a transition (note that only numerical properties and colors are changed—changes to font family or background image would occur instantly).

Usage:

```
myElement.morph(selector);
```

Example:

```
$('myElement').morph('.myCssClass');
```

When you'll use it: One of the problems with using effects to transition style properties is that you end up incorporating aspects of your design into the code that defines interaction. We have clear lines between presentation (CSS) and data (HTML), and between data (HTML) and interaction (JavaScript), but the lines between interaction (JavaScript) and design (CSS) are somewhat blurry. We use JavaScript to change the layout, and in the process we add all these CSS instructions to our code.

To a certain extent, this is unavoidable. But `Fx.Morph`'s ability to accept a CSS selector allows us to remove at least some of the CSS properties from the layout.

Note Using this functionality does not actually add the class to the element being transitioned. If you want the result of a morph operation to end with the element having the class applied, use the `chain` method:

```
myElement.morph('.myCssClass').chain(function(){
  myElement.addClass('myCssClass');
});
```

Fx.Transitions

By default, all the effects classes use a sinodal equation for their transitions, but if you include `Fx.Transitions.js`, you get several other ones that can create more expressive interactions.

The Transitions

Briefly, here are the transitions you get when you include this script:

linear

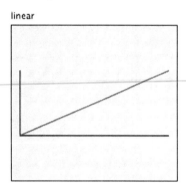

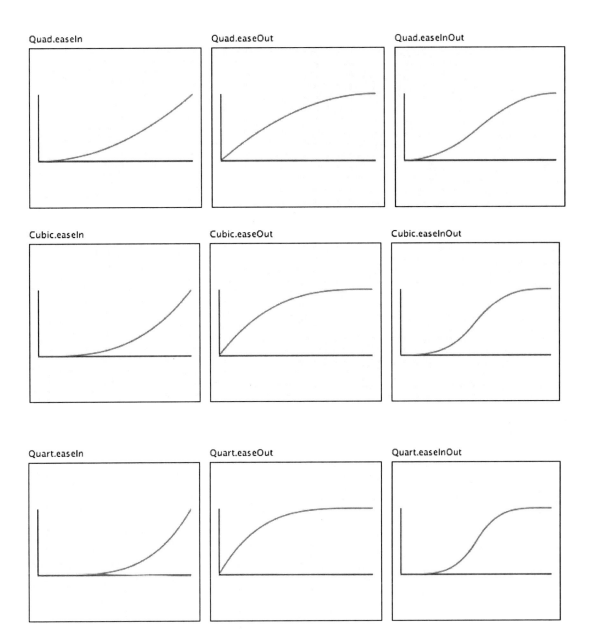

Quint.easeIn

Quint.easeOut

Quint.easeInOut

Expo.easeIn

Expo.easeOut

Expo.easeInOut

Circ.easeIn

Circ.easeOut

Circ.easeInOut

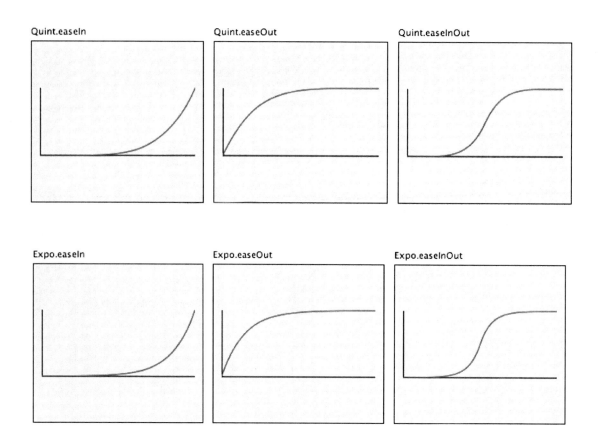

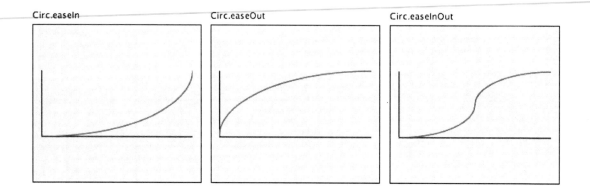

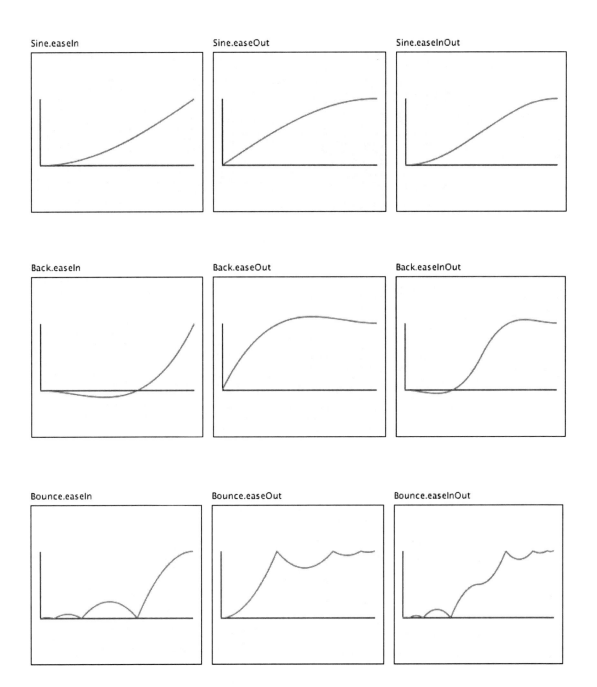

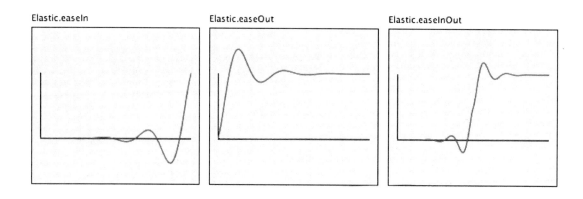

Elastic.easeIn Elastic.easeOut Elastic.easeInOut

Specifying a Transition for an Effect

When you initialize an effect, you can use the default transition
(`Liniear.easeInOut`) or you can specify any of the transitions shown in
the preceding section.

Example:

```
var effect = new Fx.Tween(myElement, {
    transition: Fx.Transitions.Elastic.easeInOut
});
```

Because this is a lot of typing to do, MooTools provides shortcuts to each
of the transitions. Here's the same thing as the preceding example, only this
time using the shorthand for the transition:

```
var effect = new Fx.Tween(myElement, {
    transition: 'elastic:in:out'
});
```

Creating Your Own Transition

If you are a hard-core math whiz, you can actually create your own
transitions. I'm not going to go into how to do this here, but I wanted to
mention it. If you're interested, look at the MooTools documentation on the
`Fx.Transition` class and then look at the source of `Fx.Transitions.js`.

The Rest of Fx.*

MooTools file organization gets rearranged periodically as our thinking on how best to organize the codebase changes and shifts. The classes and methods don't change much (and where they do a compatibility layer is provided), but the location of these things often do.

Currently, the Fx group consists solely of `Fx`, `Fx.CSS`, `Fx.Tween`, `Fx.Morph`, and `Fx.Transitions`, but these aren't the only effects classes that MooTools has to offer.

The rest are in the plug-ins group. I discuss these in greater detail in Chapter 11, but, briefly, they could be described as classes that are not fundmentally required to build a good web experience with MooTools. Classes like `Drag` or `Tips` are things that most web experiences can do without.

The same can be said of the other effects libraries:

- `Fx.Slide`: This effect slides elements in and out of view (I think of this effect like an old timey cash register that slides up the values of what you owe).

- `Fx.Scroll`: This effect is used to smoothly scroll any overflown element (including the window).

- `Fx.Elements`: This effect is used to transition numerous styles on numerous elements.

You'll see more on these in Chapter 11.

Chapter 10: Request

If there's any technology most associated with Web 2.0, it's Ajax. Short for Asynchronous JavaScript and XML, Ajax refers to the process of sending and receiving data to and from a server without reloading an entire page.

The native tools for doing this are tied up in a JavaScript object called XMLHttpRequest. Microsoft actually introduced the technology for support for Outlook Web Access 2000. In IE, it showed up as an ActiveX object called XMLHTTP. Since then it's been implemented as a native JavaScript object (called XMLHttpRequest) for every browser except Internet Explorer, which still uses the ActiveX control.

The obvious problem with these native solutions is that you have to use different objects for different browsers, but even if you look at the standard XMLHttpRequest object, the interface leaves a lot to be desired.

This is where MooTools comes to our rescue, providing us with three classes that make Ajax much more pleasant to work with: Request, Request.HTML, and Request.JSON.

Request

What it does: The Request class is for standard request/response interactions when you need to send and/or receive data to and from the server.

Usage:

```
new Request(options);
```

Example:

```
var myRequest = new Request({
  url: '/requestHandler.php',
  method: 'get',
  onSuccess: function(responseText, responseXML) {
    alert(responseText);
  }
});
myRequest.send('username=johndoe&first=john&last=doe');
//OR
myRequest.send({
  username: "johndoe",
  first: "john",
  last: "doe"
});
```

When you'll use it: Making an interactive web experience will almost always include sending information about state changes to a server and requesting new information on demand. If a user can drag and drop and reorder items in a list, you'll need to send the new order to the server for storage. If the user clicks a discussion thread to expand it and see the contents of that thread, you need to fetch that content to display it if you don't deliver it when the page loads. These kinds of interactions are increasingly part of the user's expectations.

For example, consider something as simple as rating a product on a scale of one through five stars. Users expect to be able to click the star of their choice and see that decision immediately reflected. If the page reloaded entirely, they would feel that something was off. As users continue to expect more and more interactive experiences, our use of Ajax will grow.

Note `Request` has several events that you can use in your code:

- `onSuccess`: This event is fired whenever the instance receives a successful response from the server. It is passed two arguments: `responseText` and `responseXML`.

- `onFailure`: This event is fired whenever the instance receives an unsuccessful response from the server (like 404). It is passed as its argument the instance of the request object (either `XMLHttpResponse` or the `XMLHTTP ActiveXObject` in the case of Internet Explorer).

- `onCancel`: This event is fired whenever a running request is canceled. It is not passed any arguments.

- `onException`: This event is fired whenever there is an exception when setting the headers of the `XMLHttpResponse` object.

- `onRequest`: This event is fired whenever the instance actually sends a request. It is not passed any arguments.

- `onComplete`: This event is fired whenever `onSuccess` or `onFailure` occur. It is passed the same arguments as `onSuccess` or `onFailure`.

Request Options

The `Request` class has numerous options fully outlined in the MooTools documentation. You can see a few of them illustrated in the preceding example, but it's important that you spend some time looking at the current documentation to learn about the various ways you can configure the class.

Request.send

What it does: When you create an instance of `Request`, no data is sent until you invoke its `send` method, which sends the request to the server.

Usage:

```
myRequest.send();
myRequest.send(object);
myRequest.send(queryString);
```

Example:

```
var myRequest = new Request({
  url: '/requestHandler.php',
  method: 'get',
  data: {
    layout: 'compact'
  }
});
//Send the default data, layout=compact:
myRequest.send();
//Overwrite the data default:
myRequest.send({layout: 'extended'});
```

When you'll use it: This method accepts as an optional argument the data to include in the request. There is also a `data` option when you instantiate the class where you can specify default information. This gives you the ability to reuse an instance of `Request` repeatedly, sending different information with each request.

Why would you want to reuse the class? Well, for instance, you can set the `link` option to "cancel" so that you can let the user initiate numerous requests but only use the last one. Consider an interface where users can filter data by checking check boxes. Each time they click your code requests new, filtered information from the server. By reusing the request and canceling previous requests, you can fetch only the most recent state that the user has created.

Request: .get, .post, .put, .delete

The `Request` class offers shortcut methods that work just like `Request.send` except that they use different "method" arguments in the request. Also, these shortcuts can accept an optional first argument for the URL.

Examples:

```
//Send the request as a "get":
myRequest.get({username: 'johndoe'});
//Send the request as a "post":
myRequest.post({username: 'johndoe'});
//Send the request as a "put":
myRequest.put({username: 'johndoe'});
//Send the request as a "delete":
myRequest.delete({username: 'johndoe'});
//Each of these can take a url, too:
myRequest.delete('/delete_user', {username: 'johndoe'});
```

Request.cancel

What it does: This method simply cancels a running request.

Usage:

```
myRequest.cancel();
```

When you'll use it: As illustrated in the earlier section "Request.send," there are times when you need to stop listening for a response and instead send a new state to the server. By canceling the request, you'll prevent the `onSuccess`, `onFailure`, and `onComplete` events from firing. So, for example, if you have an effect that displays a message that a user's changes have been set to occur `onSuccess`, and the user makes a change followed by another quick change before the first one has received a response, you can cancel the first request and send a new instruction. Your message will only display when the second one returns.

Note   This does NOT cancel the request to the server. Rather, it instructs the client (the browser) to stop listening for a response. So, for example, if a user clicks "delete" on an item, and you send a request to the server to remove something from that user's account, you can stop listening for the server to respond to this request, but the server has already been sent the instruction.

Element.send

What it does: MooTools integrates a shortcut into the `Element` prototype to make it easy to send information based on the contents of any DOM element that contains input elements (typically a form).

Usage:

```
$('myForm').send(url);
```

Example:

```
$('myForm').set('send', {
  onSuccess: function(response){
    alert(response);
  }
}).addEvent('submit', function(event){
  event.preventDefault();
  this.send(); //Uses the URL from "action"
});
```

When you'll use it: Like all the `Element` methods that allow you to invoke a class (as with the effects shortcuts), this just saves you keystrokes. When you use this method on a form, the parameters of the form (the method and the URL) and all the input values are used just as if the form had been submitted. The only difference is that the data is sent with Ajax.

Using Element.set with Element.send

As with the other shortcuts (as discussed previously in Chapter 9), you can get at the "built-in" instance of `Request` using `Element.get` and `Element.set`. This will allow you to set the default state for that instance.

Example:

```
//Set a default value for this element's
//Request instance:
myElement.set('send', {method: 'post'});
//Retrieve this element's Request instance
//and cancel it:
myElement.get('send').cancel();
```

Request.HTML

What it does: This extension to the `Request` class automates updating the content of a DOM element with the response of an Ajax request.

Usage:

```
new Request.HTML(options);
```

Example:

```
new Request.HTML({
  url: '/userprofile.php',
  data: {
    userid: '1001'
  },
  update: $('userProfileDiv');
}).send();
```

When you'll use it: A very common pattern implied by the Web 2.0 buzzword is the use of Ajax to fetch display data from the server on demand. If a user expands a section of content, rather than have that content loaded and hidden, it's fashionable to instead go get the layout that belongs there only if and when the user requests it.

There are some trade-offs to this practice. It means that this content is not visible to search engines, for example. But for the most part I encourage this practice. When used well, it can increase load times for the user and allow for a page to present a lot more information that the user can drill down into quickly.

Element.load

What it does: As with `Element.send`, which essentially posts a form via Ajax, this method allows you to update the contents of a DOM element quickly with minimal code.

Usage:

```
$('myElement').load(url[, data]);
```

Example:

```
$('myElement').load('/page2.html');
```

When you'll use it: This handy shortcut allows you to acquire any element from the DOM and update its content via Ajax. It's very short and easy to read and understand, and you'll likely find yourself using it more often than typing out `new Request.HTML...` etc.

Request.JSON

What it does: This class automates the sending and receiving of JSON information (see "JSON" in Chapter 6).

Usage:

```
new Request.JSON(options);
```

Example:

```
//This code will send a data object via a
//GET request and alert the retrieved data.
var jsonRequest = new Request.JSON({
  url: " /tellMeAge.php",
  onComplete: function(person){
    alert(person.age);     //Alerts "25 years".
    alert(person.height); //Alerts "170 cm".
    alert(person.weight); //Alerts "120 kg".
  }
}).get({'firstName': 'John', 'lastName': 'Doe'});
```

When you'll use it: As outlined in Chapter 6, JSON is a transport language much like XML, except that it uses native JavaScript notation. Using XML to transport the data in and out of JavaScript requires you to crawl up and down a document tree, while using JSON allows you to use dot notation (as illustrated previously). Despite it being the "x" in Ajax, it's actually increasingly rare to use XML to manage data transactions from the browser to the server.

Chapter 11: Plug-Ins

MooTools, at its heart, is focused on making JavaScript more pleasant to write. Making it easier to write well-designed code encourages reuse, flexibility, and object-oriented principles.

Included in the library are several files that aren't really part of this core mission. These files certainly allow for interesting interfaces with drag and drop, sortable lists, tooltips and more, but they aren't really what MooTools, to date, has considered its core mission.

This is why they are all lumped together and described as "plug-ins." In Chapter 12, I talk about plug-ins available from third parties. It is the modular nature of MooTools itself that allows for the creation of plug-ins with relative ease, and while MooTools contains many files it considers plug-ins, this assignation should not imply that they aren't great additions to the library, nor that writing your own plug-ins is something you should avoid. MooTools was built for extensibility, and to that end it illustrates how to do it with its own plug-ins.

A More General Overview

Now that you've seen how to write classes and how to use them, I'm going to spend a little less time on the classes in these next chapters than I have in the previous ones. By now, you should have the hang of how to initialize a class and pass it arguments and options, and how to invoke the methods of that class and integrate those methods with actions and events on your site.

Consequently, I'm going to give an overview of all the MooTools plug-ins here, but for the most part I'm going to direct you to the online documentation and the demos of these classes so that you can see them in action in the browser, so I can spend more pages here on real-world examples (beginning in Chapter 13).

Assets

The `Assets` set of classes automate the injection of assets into the document (style sheets, images, JavaScript tags, etc.). Unless you're doing a lot of this in your document(s), it's usually not worth using this script and including its download weight. If you are injecting only one or two things, you'll do better to just use the `Element` constructor and injection methods.

The `javascript` and `css` methods all return an element object that has *already* been injected into the document.

Assets.javascript

This is pretty straightforward:

```
var myScript = new Asset.javascript('/myscript.js', {
  onload: function() {
    //Call a function from myscripts.js
    MyScript.start();
  }
});
```

Assets.css

Pretty much the same thing as the preceding JavaScript example:

```
var myCSS = new Asset.css('/mycss.css');
```

Assets.image

Unlike the `Assets.css` and `Assets.javascript` methods, this method does *not* inject the image into the document. It does, however, preload the image.

```
var myImage = new Asset.image('/myImg.gif', {
  onload: function() {
    //Image is loaded and you can read the dimensions.
    //We resize it when it is bigger than 120px.
    if (this.height > 120) this.height = 120;
    if (this.width > 120) this.width = 120;
    this.inject('gallery');
  }
});
```

Assets.images

This class just takes an array of URLs and returns an array of image elements.

```
var myImages = new Asset.images([
  '/images/myImage.png',
  '/images/myImage2.gif'
], {
  onProgress: function(counter, index){
    alert(counter + ' image loaded ...');
  },
  onComplete: function(){
    alert('All images loaded!');
  }
});
```

Accordion

The Accordion, for better or worse, is perhaps the interface effect most associated with MooTools. This is probably because the original Moo.Fx library (a 3KB add-on to Prototype.js) included it, and, at the time, few other libraries had anything like it (to my knowledge). Indeed, if you visit the Moo.Fx page (http://moofx.mad4milk.net/), you'll see the Accordion is still in use.

The way the interface works is that it takes a list of items and headers and hides all but one of the items. When the user clicks a different header, it simultaneously collapses the currently visible section while expanding the section that corresponds to the clicked header.

Example:

```
new Accordion($$('dl#accordionExample dt'),
              $$('dl#accordionExample dd'));
```

The first section displayed:

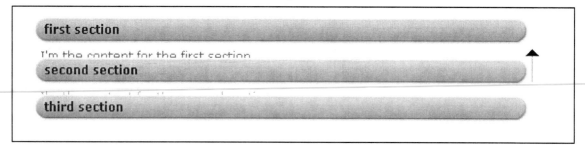

The second section, when clicked, expands as the first section closes:

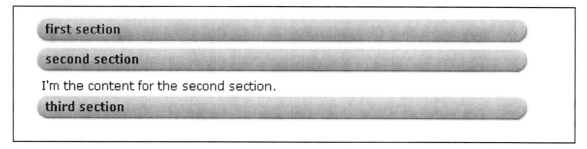

The completed transition:

Fx.Slide

This class slides the contents of an element in and out of view. It only allows for sliding *down* like a window blind or sliding in from the left.

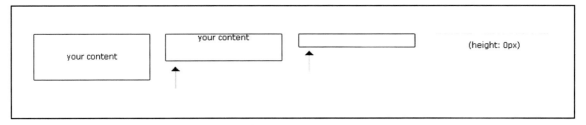

It accomplishes this by wrapping your content inside another div whose overflow is hidden, and then moving the offset of your content negatively up or to the left to "slide" it out.

Example:

```
var mySlide = new Fx.Slide($('myDiv'), {duration: 200});
mySlide.slideOut(); //My element slides out of view
//mySlide.toggle will slide back in now because it
//was hidden:
mySlide.toggle();
```

Fx.Scroll

This class smoothly scrolls the contents of any overflowed element (e.g., an element with scrollbars), including the window. You can use it to smoothly scroll back to the top of a window, to scroll to any x/y location, or to scroll to any element on the page.

Example:

```
var myScrollFx = new Fx.Scroll(document.body);
//Scroll to 300px from the top of the page:
myScrollFx.start(0, 300);
//Scroll down to the specified element:
myScrollFx.toElement($('myDiv'));
//Scroll to the top of the page:
myScrollFx.toTop();
```

Fx.Elements

This effects class works kind of like `Fx.Morph` in that it lets you alter numerous CSS properties at once; however, in addition to this, it allows you to alter numerous properties *on numerous elements* at once. If you want to fade out three elements, while moving two others and fading out another three, `Fx.Elements` will handle this transition more smoothly than if you used `Fx.Tween` or `Fx.Morph` for each element.

Example:

```
var myFx = new Fx.Elements($$('div.animated'));
//Let's say there are 3 of these div.animated objects
myFx.start({
  '0': { //Animate the first one from a spec to a square
    height: [0, 100],
    width: [0, 100]
  },
  '1': { //Resize the second one from a square to a spec
    height: [100, 0],
    width: [100, 0]
  },
  '2': { //Fade the third out to zero
    opacity: 0
  }
});
```

Drag

The `Drag` class automates the work of tracking the movement of the mouse and relating that movement to some value. Using `Drag`, you could alter the color of the background of an element based on where the mouse moved. You could alter the thickness of a border or iterate a counter up or down. Its numerous options and events allow you to create any interaction based on mouse movement that you can imagine.

Example:

```
//Create an Adobe Reader-style drag-to-scroll container
//that moves the contents of the page as the user drags
var myDragScroller = new Drag('myContainer', {
    style: false, //Disable dragging by left/top style
    invert: true,
    modifiers: {x: 'scrollLeft', y: 'scrollTop'}
});
```

Element.makeResizeable

The only shortcut that comes with `Drag.js` is to make an element resizable. Using this, you can allow the user to grab an element and drag to make it wider, taller, or both. You can specify a "handle" that the user has to click and drag. Otherwise, the user can click anywhere inside the element and drag, and the element will resize.

Example:

```
$('myDiv').makeResizeable({
    //An element inside acts as handle, not the whole div:
    handle: $('myHandle'),
    //The user can only resize vertically
    modifiers: {x: false, y: 'height'} });
```

Drag.Move

This class automates the interface interaction of dragging objects around. It extends Drag to manage the process of relocating an element relative to the movement of the mouse.

It has all the same options as Drag with the addition of two very useful new ones:

- container: A DOM element that the draggable element should be constrained to; this will prevent the user from dragging the element outside of a certain space.

- droppables: A collection of DOM elements that are OK for the user to drop the dragged element into. The events "over", "leave", and "drop" get fired on the class with the dragged element as first argument when the dragged element hovers, leaves, or get dropped on the droppable.

Example:

```
var myDrag = new Drag.Move('draggable', {
    droppables: '.droppable',
    onDrop: function(element, droppable){
        if (!droppable)
           console.log(element, ' dropped on nothing');
        else
           console.log(element, 'dropped on', droppable);
    },
    onEnter: function(element, droppable){
        console.log(element, 'entered', droppable);
    },
    onLeave: function(element, droppable){
        console.log(element, 'left', droppable);
    }
});
```

Element.makeDraggable

This is a shortcut method for making an element draggable. It accepts the same arguments as `Drag.Move`.

Example:

```
$('myElement').makeDraggable({
    droppables: '.droppable',
    onDrop: function(element, droppable){ ... },
    onEnter: function(element, droppable) { ... },
    onLeave: function(element, droppable) { ... }
});
```

Color

The `Color` class is a utility plug-in that's useful in altering color values. Using it, you can add and subtract color values, making a given color lighter or darker by mixing it with another color value. I personally don't find myself using it that much, but if you have a design that requires a programatically defined color palette, this class can help you automate calculating color values.

Group

This utility class allows you to group numerous items together and attach events to them as a collection. For instance, if you want something to happen only after the user has clicked numerous items, or if you want something to happen when numerous Ajax requests complete, you can group the objects together and attach a single event to the group.

Example:

```
var xhr1 = new Request('/one.js', {
  evalResponse: true
});
var xhr2 = new Request('abstraction.js', {
  evalResponse: true
});
var xhr3 = new Request('template.js', {
  evalResponse: true
});

var group = new Group(xhr1, xhr2, xhr3);
group.addEvent('onComplete', function(){
    alert('All Scripts loaded');
});

xhr1.request();
xhr2.request();
xhr3.request();
//When all three complete, the alert will display
```

Hash.Cookie

I know what you're thinking. You're thinking about hash cookies. Well, I hate to disappoint, but this class won't give you a case of the munchies *and* satisfy them. This combination of `Cookie` and `Hash` automates the creation of a cookie containing a set of key values. It encodes the object into a query string value (a JSON string, to be precise) and then evaluates it on retrieval. This is more appropriate than having several cookies for storing user preferences and the like, though it has the limitation of only supporting a fixed amount of data (4KB is the limit).

Example:

```
var fruits = new Hash.Cookie('fruit-colors', {
  duration: 3600,
  path: "/",
  autoSave: true //Save on every operation
});
fruits.extend({
    'lemon': 'yellow',
    'apple': 'red'
});
fruits.set('melon', 'green');
fruits.get('lemon'); //yellow

// ... On another page ... values load automatically

var fruits = new Hash.Cookie('fruit-colors', {
  duration: 365,
  path: "/"
});
fruits.get('melon'); //green

fruits.erase(); // Delete cookie
```

Sortables

If you have a list that you need to allow the user to reorder, the Sortables class takes most of the work out of the process for you. While it does automate all the interaction and dragging and whatnot, it doesn't actually send any data anywhere as a result of the user changing the order. You'll have to integrate something like the Request class to send stateful instructions back to the server for storage.

The Sortables class allows you to drag and drop inside a single list or across several. This way users can reorder a single list, or reorder items across lists with ease. You control this distinction by passing in a single list element container or several.

This class has many options, which allows it to be very flexible. The examples on MooTools.net and in the online companion to this book (`http://www.mootorial.com`) illustrate some of the ways you can configure the class.

Example:

```
var mySortables = new Sortables('#list-1, #list-2', {
  constrain: true,
  revert: true,
  onComplete: function(){
    new Request({
      url: '/dragManager.php'
    }).post({
      newOrder: this.serialize()
    });
  }
});
```

Slider

Thought it's not that commonly used on the Web, the slider is certainly a recognizable interface element appearing in desktop apps, the iPhone, and car dashboards. MooTools gives us an easy class to drop in when we want to implement this interface element into our own applications. The element consists of a knob (that is dragged left-right or up-down) and the element that contains (and therefore constrains) it. You can specify how many steps are in the range and what happens when the user moves the knob.

4

Scroller

This class will scroll the contents of any overflowed element (including the window) when the mouse approaches the edge of that element. This is very useful for drag-and-drop applications. If the user can drag an object from one place to another, but the destination is out of view because it is scrolled above or below, then you need some way for the user whose mouse is engaged in dragging the item to scroll the window.

Consequently, this class is typically used in conjunction with Drag and Drag.Move.

Tips

The Tips class automates tooltips. Give your elements a title property for the title of the tip and a rel property for the description, and then instantiate the Tips class.

Example:

```
<a href="/foo.html" title="The Foo Page"
    rel="This link goes to the Foo Page"
    class="tip">Go to Foo</a>
```

Code:

```
new Tips($$('a.tip'));
```

Result:

Chapter 12: Third-Party Plug-Ins

As stated at the beginning of the previous chapter, the MooTools framework has, to date, focused mainly on the core challenge of making it easy and pleasant to write good JavaScript. While it contains a healthy number of useful plug-ins, the framework itself is designed for extensibility.

Consequently, numerous plug-ins are available on the Web for you to download and use. Most of the plug-ins that are well written and well documented follow all the patterns and conventions outlined in the previous chapters. These plug-ins tend to provide a lot of options and events to configure them, but regardless they are almost always classes that can be extended and altered.

The CNET Clientside Libraries

For the last few years, I've been the principal JavaScript developer at CNET Networks (despite the fact that my role there was never officially as an engineer—I was a product manager). I left CNET in the fall of 2007 to pursue my own startup, but I continue to contribute to the codebase that I authored as well as blog about JavaScript and MooTools at `http://clientside.cnet.com`.

During the period that I spent authoring a lot of this code (and contributing to MooTools), we at CNET decided to release as much of our JavaScript as possible, and as a result we have a large number of plug-ins that have been thoroughly tested and put into production on a heavily trafficked network.

Here is a brief overview of *some* of the files that can be found there to date. You can visit these libraries by going to the following URLs:

`http://clientside.cnet.com/js`	Download the JavaScript libraries.
`http://clientside.cnet.com/docs`	View the documentation.
`http://clientside.cnet.com/wiki`	See working code examples of all the classes.

dbug

This wrapper for the Firebug console allows you to leave debug lines in your code and "turn them on" only when you need them. In addition to allowing you to leave information for yourself to inspect when something goes wrong, it helps prevent the accidental publishing of code that contains `console` instructions that will break in browsers without Firebug.

Browser.Extras

This extension adds numerous methods for managing URL data as well as a class for launching pop-up windows.

Native Extensions

You'll find extensions to `String` and `Hash` as well as a native `Date` object that includes string parsing and date formatting methods.

Element Extensions

You'll find methods for selecting text in form elements, computing the actual size of elements, positioning elements relative to other elements, and shortcuts like `Element.hide` and `Element.show`.

Effects Extensions

`Fx.Reveal` will automatically and smoothly transition an element whose display style is set to "none" to "block", expanding the element and fading it in. It's a less abrupt method than just changing the display from "none" to "block" (or vice versa).

`Fx.Move` allows you to move an element from one location to a location relative to another (e.g., move this element on top of, or below, or to the right of some other element).

`Fx.Sort` allows you to reorder a list of elements smoothly; they all move to their new locations instead of just jumping to them.

`Fx.Marquee` helps automate a marquee effect so you can repeatedly show messages with different transitions.

Request

The `JsonP` class allows you to send and receive data to a remote server on a different domain, a limitation that Ajax doesn't allow. This has the potential to be insecure, so you should be sure to send and receive data to and from servers that you control and trust.

UI

The CNET Clientside Libraries have over a dozen interface classes, including the following:

- `IconMenu`: An icon carousel that allows the user to paginate through a horizontal or vertical list of items.

- `Modalizer`: A class that creates a "modal" layer that overlays the contents of the window with a semitransparent layer; this is integrated with our `StickyWin` class, detailed later in this list, to create dialogs that gray out the page content until they interact with the dialog.

- `PopupDetails`: A class that creates an interface of tooltip-like displays with rich details. For instance, if you have a lot of products displayed, you can show rich metadata when the user mouses over the image of the product.

- `StickyWin.alert`: A replacement for `alert()` that looks a little nicer and doesn't freeze the browser.

- `StickyWin`: An in-page DHTML pop-up manager for pop-up messages and forms. This highly configurable and flexible, draggable, resizable UI element can be used for nearly any pop-up interaction.

- `Waiter`: A class that overlays a DOM element with a semitransparent layer and a spinning Ajax indicator to illustrate to users that there is some sort of transaction occurring that they must wait for. The class can be used on its own, but it is also integrated into the `Request` classes so that you can enable it with a single option passed when you create a `Request` instance. When the request is running, the waiter is displayed.

Layout

The CNET Clientside Libraries feature a few classes designed to animate layouts or facilitate creating them on the fly (like data tables).

- `HtmlTable`: This automates the building of an HTML table from a data set, allowing you to add rows on the fly.

- `MultipleOpenAccordion`: This is very similar to the `Accordion` class in MooTools except that it allows the user to open more than one section at a time.

- `MooScroller`: This class re-creates the traditional scroll interface for overflowed elements using DOM elements that can be styled.

- `SimpleCarousel`: This class offers a simple carousel interface with slides and buttons that show the corresponding slide. It can also automatically cycle through the slides until the user interacts with it.

- `SimpleSlideShow`: This class creates a simple slide show with previous and next buttons.

- `TabSwapper`: A common interface element, the "tabbed box" allows users to click tabs above a set of content elements to see the corresponding element.

Forms

CNET builds a lot of internal tools, and consequently we have a lot of JavaScript tools for making managing content more pleasant. Here are a few of them:

- `DatePicker`: A flexible date selector that lets the user choose from a calendar of dates, this class can be configured to allow for selecting a single date or a date range, as well as entering a specific time.

- `FormValidator`: This class is a nonintrusive form validator. After assigning the inputs of a form various CSS classes, you can instantiate this class to give validation errors to users as they interact with the form, saving them the trouble of having to submit the form to get errors. It also allows for custom validation rules.

- `OverText`: This class will take the alt or title text for an input and display it over the element when it has no value. This allows you to give a contextual element to empty inputs. When the user clicks into the element, the text is hidden. If the user clicks out without entering any values, the text returns. The text itself is a DOM element positioned above the input that can be styled however you like. It is not actual input text, so it won't be submitted accidentally by the form.

- `SimpleEditor`: This class creates a simple HTML editor. It is not a WYSIWYG editor, but instead offers buttons to wrap selected text with HTML tags or else prompts the user to fill out the attributes of a tag (like an image tag).

This isn't a complete accounting of all the scripts Clientside has to offer, but it should give you an idea of what's there.

Other Third-Party Scripts

The collection of CNET's Clientside scripts I outlined in the previous section aren't the only plug-ins available. There are numerous other authors out there who have released plug-ins. Most of these plug-ins can be found by visiting the MooTools forums (`http://forum.mootools.net`) and browsing to the "Your Scripts" category. Here various users have submitted their own scripts for members of the MooTools community to use and provide feedback.

Some of these are hit or miss. A good indication of a good script is how well documented it is and whether it has numerous examples that you can see in action.

Note   As of this writing, the MooTools forums have moved to a Google Group (`http://groups.google.com/group/mootools-users`). The old forum, however, is still there (in read-only mode) and features all the scripts I refer to earlier, so it's still worth digging into. The MooTools team is currently working on a plug-in page to feature other third-party plug-ins, so check the MooTools site for updates.

Of the scripts available in this section, I have used only a few, described next.

Autocompleter, FancyUpload, ReMooz, SqueezeBox, Roar

Harald Kirschner (a.k.a. digitarald) is another contributor to MooTools and has numerous plug-ins up on his site (`http://digitarald.de`). There you can find the following classes, all of which I recommend trying out:

- `Autocompleter`: This is an autocompletion class that works with local data in memory (e.g., an object defined in the page), Ajax, or JSON. Note that I have integrated CNET's `JsonP` class with `Autocompleter` and provided a copy in the CNET libraries. I've also documented all the options which, as of this writing, Harald hasn't gotten around to yet.

- `FancyUpload`: Swiff and Ajax come together for an elegant upload interface that displays the progress of any number of files being uploaded to the server.

- `ReMooz`: This image gallery–like plug-in lets users zoom in on thumbnails and get a high-quality version of the image.

- `Roar Notifications`: This notification widget streamlines incoming messages for updates or errors, adding only minimal distraction to the interface.

- `SqueezeBox`: This Lightbox-inspired pop-up allows you to embed just about anything from images to Flash videos in an in-page pop-up.

- `History`: This class adds back-button functionality to Ajax-applications. It provides a history-change event and a dynamic routing to manage several widgets in one page.

Slimbox

This is a clone of Lightbox, a slide show built for script.aculo.us and Prototype (`http://www.lokeshdhakar.com/projects/lightbox2/`). The original port of Lightbox into `Slimbox` (`http://www.digitalia.be/software/slimbox`) was basically a code conversion to MooTools syntax (with a refactoring of the effects queue and other parts), but it didn't actually create a MooTools class out of it. Instead, it works like the Prototype version does, which is a collection of methods into the `Lightbox` namespace.

The downside of this conversion is that it's not a class, so it's not possible to have more than one instance, it doesn't have configurable options or events, and you can't extend it.

Finally, the other issue with the library is that it hasn't been updated for MooTools 1.2 by the original converter. Consequently, you'll find a new version in CNET's library that does all this, though the credit for it all still belongs to the original author of Lightbox, Lokesh Dhakar (who wrote Lightbox for Prototype.js) and Christophe Beyl (who first ported it to MooTools).

. . . And More

I don't spend a lot of my time digging around in the forums for plug-ins that people post, but there are a lot of them to play around with. If you're looking for something that seems like the kind of thing someone else would have made (date pickers, form validators, pop-ups, etc.), chances are someone did. Actually, chances are that several people did and there are several versions for you to choose from, so I encourage you to dig around in the "Your Scripts" section of the MooTools forum when you have the time.

Chapter 13: Real-World Examples

The bulk of this book up to this point is designed to help you learn the purpose of various methods and classes in the MooTools library. It's possible, through reading about these methods and classes and looking at the examples, to glean the "MooTools way" of doing things. As outlined at the beginning of this book in "About MooTools" in the Introduction, the following goals are part of MooTools's core mission:

- Don't duplicate code.
- Add functionality that fits in principle with JavaScript's own design philosophy.
- Extend native objects (`String`, `Function`, `Array`, `Element`, `Event`, and `Number`) as JavaScript was designed to do.
- Write clean, clear, well-named code that is understandable when read by anyone with the skills to understand it.
- Abstract as much away from the browser as possible.
- Whenever possible, make it still feel like you're writing JavaScript.
- Make it modular.

These aren't all the points outlined in the Introduction, but they are the pertinent points to what I'm going to cover next: the code you write.

MooTools is a framework that makes authoring JavaScript easier and better in many ways, but you still need to write your own code to add functionality to your pages. If you include the MooTools library on your pages, absolutely nothing will happen unless you write code creating instances of effects, Ajax, and more.

So let's take on some real-world examples of how to author JavaScript in a "MooTools way."

A Simple Page

As the section "Adding MooTools to Your Page(s)" in Chapter 1 illustrates, adding the MooTools library to your pages is pretty straightfoward. You download the library and save it to the directory with the rest of your web assets and then reference it with a `script` tag:

```
<!DOCTYPE html PUBLIC "-//W3C//DTD XHTML 1.0 Strict//EN"
  "http://www.w3.org/TR/xhtml1/DTD/xhtml1-strict.dtd">
<html xmlns="http://www.w3.org/1999/xhtml" xml:lang="en"
  lang="en" dir="ltr">
  <head>
    <meta http-equiv="Content-Type"
     content="text/html; charset=UTF-8" />
    <title>Your title</title>
    <script type="text/JavaScript"
     src="MooTools.js"></script>
    <script type="text/JavaScript"
     src="yourSiteCode.js"></script>
    <script type="text/JavaScript">
      //Or write some code inline
    </script>
  </head>
  <body>....</body>
</html>
```

Let's imagine that we want to attach a simple event to all the links on the page to load the content each points to into a container. In this example, we can see the `DomReady` custom event (see Chapter 6) in use, the `get` and `addEvent` element methods (see Chapter 5) in use, an instance of `Request` (see Chapter 10) to fetch data from the server, the native `Event` class (see Chapter 4) to stop the link clicks, as well as selectors (see Chapter 6) and array iteration (see Chapter 4). We'll pick apart the code line by line after the full example that follows.

```
<!DOCTYPE html PUBLIC "-//W3C//DTD XHTML 1.0 Strict//EN"
  "http://www.w3.org/TR/xhtml1/DTD/xhtml1-strict.dtd">
<html xmlns="http://www.w3.org/1999/xhtml" xml:lang="en"
  lang="en" dir="ltr">
  <head>
    <meta http-equiv="Content-Type"
     content="text/html; charset=UTF-8" />
    <title>Your title</title>
    <script type="text/JavaScript"
     src="MooTools.js"></script>
    <script type="text/JavaScript"
     src="yourSiteCode.js"></script>
    <script type="text/JavaScript">
      window.addEvent('domready', function(){
        $$('#pageLinks a').each(function(link){
          link.addEvent('click', function(event){
            event.preventDefault();
            $('pageContainer').load(link.get('href'));
            //you could also express the above as:
            //$('pageContainer').load(this.get('href'));
            //as "this" here is the link
          });
        });
      });
    </script>
  </head>
  <body>
    <ul id="pageLinks">
      <li><a href="/page1.html">page 1</a></li>
      <li><a href="/page2.html">page 2</a></li>
      <li><a href="/page3.html">page 3</a></li>
      <li><a href="/page4.html">page 4</a></li>
    </ul>
    <div id="pageContainer"></div>
  </body>
</html>
```

Dissecting the Example

Let's look at the preceding example line by line. I'm only going to focus on the JavaScript, as the HTML is pretty straightforward.

First, we can't reference anything in the DOM until it's there, and our `script` tag, at the top of the page in the `head`, will be interpreted before the rest of the HTML loads. We use the `addEvent` method on the `window` to wrap our functionality in the `DomReady` event so that our code will be executed as soon as the HTML is loaded (but it won't have to wait for images and whatnot to load).

```
window.addEvent('domready', function(){
```

Now that it's safe to reference the DOM, we can select the links we want to modify. We use the `$$` method to select all the links in the `pageLinks` div. We'll need `Selectors.js` in order for this to work because `$$` accepts only tag names unless you include this script in your copy of MooTools. With it you can specify a CSS selector.

```
$$('#pageLinks a').each(function(link){
//Can be also written as
$('pageLinks').getElements('a').each(...
```

Here we see an example of *function chaining*. This is when we execute a method on the object returned by another function (this shouldn't be confused with the `Chain` class). All this means is that if a function returns a string, you can invoke the function and then execute a `string` method on the result. For example, `$('myElement').setStyle(...)` invokes the `$` method and then invokes the `setStyle` method on the element returned by it. `setStyle` is a property of `Element`, not of `$`. So in the preceding example, we invoke `$$`, which always returns an array (even an empty one if it doesn't find any elements that match the selector), and then we invoke `.each`, which is a property of `Array`.

`Array.each` accepts two arguments: the item in the array being iterated over and the index of that item in the array. In our example, we don't need to reference the index, so we don't have to declare it, but we could if we wanted to.

Next, we take the link that is passed to our function and add an event to it for when the user clicks it:

```
link.addEvent('click', function(event){
```

We specify which event to monitor (`click`) and pass a function to be executed when the user clicks it. This function is anonymous (i.e., it is not declared as a variable with a name, it's just a literal `function(){}` object) and accepts as its argument the event that is created when the user clicks the link. This is an instance of the `Event` class.

Next, we prevent that event from doing what would normally happen if the user were to click the link (i.e., the page would load the URL as a new document). We don't want this to happen; we want to update a portion of the page with the contents of the URL that the link points to, so we use the `preventDefault` method so that the link click doesn't load a new page.

```
event.preventDefault();
```

Finally, when the user clicks the link, we want to update the div that holds our page information with the contents of that URL. We could create a new instance of `Request` to update the content, but the element shortcut `load` will work just fine here; no need to write more code than we need. This method accepts a URL that we need to retrieve from the link, which we do with `element.get`.

```
        $('pageContainer').load(link.get('href'));
      }); //End the addEvent statement
    }); //End the each iteration
  }); //End the domready statement
```

Note   Whenever you load content into a page this way, the URLs you request should not be entire documents; they shouldn't have head and body tags but instead should be HTML fragments. Whatever is returned by these URLs will be injected in their entirety into the document. This means that if your site has a logo and navigation bar layout, and the links you point to also have this, you'll see those elements loaded into your container. This is why you should just return the content that you would want to exist in the updated DOM container and nothing else.

Summary

This simple example strings together numerous native methods (`Element.addEvent`, `Element.get`, `Element.load`, `Array.each`, and `Event.preventDefault`), stand-alone methods (`$$`), and classes (`Request`) to add some nice functionality to our pages—all in just eight lines of readable code.

But adding functionality in this manner will only get you so far, which is why you need to write classes. You'll see an example of how to do so in the next chapter.

Chapter 14: Writing a Tab Class

In the example in Chapter 13, we had some HTML with four links to different pages, followed by a container that would display the contents of the pages those links pointed to. We implemented the previous example to select a specific group of links on a specific page, but what if our site had lots of these things? What if we had a dozen pages, each with three or four different placements of this layout? Writing the same chunk of code over and over again wouldn't be very efficient.

Instead, we should turn the pattern into a class, which we can initialize over and over again for each placement, passing in only the variables that make each one unique.

By making a piece of interaction into a class, we can maintain a state and a reference to various objects for effects, Ajax, or DOM elements. We can define methods that we can use to manipulate that state whenever we like. Finally, the resulting chunk of functionality can be extended to add more functionality later. All this adds up to resuable code that can save us a lot of time. For example, if you find a bug in your code, you fix it in one place, and every place that uses it is fixed, so you don't have to hunt down all the places where you've written the functionality and fix it in each one.

So let's write a class for the pattern we have in our example from Chapter 13. Our objective here will be to end up with the exact same result, but instead we'll be able to reuse it and extend it.

Step 1: Creating an Empty Class

When writing a class, you'll almost always start out the same way:

```
var AjaxTabs = new Class({
   Implements: [Options, Events],
   options: {},
   initialize: function(){}
});
```

This template is the very basics of a class. Any class that you're going to use more than once is going to have options (see Chapter 8), and any class that the user can interact with (or otherwise has functionality that happens at arbitrary times—like effects or Ajax) will likely have events. Any class that should do something when you instantiate it will have an `initialize` method.

Because we started out this excercise with the specific goal of reproducing our example from the previous class, I'm going to remove the options and events lines from this example, but they'll show up again as we progress. This leaves us with the following:

```
var AjaxTabs = new Class({
   initialize: function(){
   }
});
```

Step 2: Defining Arguments

In our case, we can start off knowing what the variables are by looking at the example we're trying to emulate from the previous chapter. We know we'll have links to different HTML fragments (the "pages") as well as a container where those fragments go. Our class can't work without these things, so we'll make them arguments.

This is the key distinction between arguments and options: options are just that—optional—while arguments are required for the class to work.

Sticking with this pattern will help anyone else who uses this class understand the distinction (and it'll help you, too, when you use it again after a few months pass). Being consistent with arguments versus options make it less likely that your class will break when someone else uses it.

So let's change our template by adding our arguments and storing them. I've emphasized the changes in bold here, which we'll dissect after the example. Again, we won't have options in this example yet, but they'll show up later.

```
var AjaxTabs = new Class({
   initialize: function(container, links){
      this.container = $(container);
      this.links = $$(links);
   }
});
```

The bold changes now specify that our class accepts two options: a container (where the updated content goes) and links (the page links).

Dissecting this a bit, we have the following:

First, we store the container reference as a property of the class. This way we can reference it later. We also wrap the reference with the $ method. This serves several purposes: it allows the user to pass in an element's ID (a string) or the element reference itself. It also ensures that that element is properly extended with MooTools methods.

```
      this.container = $(container);
```

Then we store the links. This array of links gets passed through $$, which serves the same purpose as the previous line being passed through $. The user can pass in an array of links or a selector to retrieve those links. If the user passes in an array of elements, we ensure that this array of elements is extended with MooTools by passing it through $$. In both cases, it won't matter if the elements have already been passed through $$ or $ there's no real expense to doing it twice.

```
this.links = $$(links);
```

So now our class can be initialized, and the values stored in it can be referenced. If we did create an instance now, it wouldn't do anything except store these references. Here's what that would look like:

```
var myAjaxTabs = new AjaxTabs($('pageContainer'),
  $$('#pageLinks a'));
myAjaxTabs.container //The $('pageContainer') div
myAjaxTabs.links //The four $$('#pageLinks a')
               //link elements
```

Now we need to actually do something with this information.

Step 3: Defining Methods

Our class now has stored references to the container and the links, but we need to actually add some behavior to them in order for our class to actually have an effect. Let's add some methods to our class.

```
var AjaxTabs = new Class({
  initialize: function(container, links){
    this.container = $(container);
    this.links = $$(links);
    this.attach();
  },
  attach: function(){
    this.links.each(function(link){
      link.addEvent('click', function(event){
        event.preventDefault();
        this.container.load(link.get('href'));
      }.bind(this));
    }, this);
  }
});
```

Cool. Now we have a class that, when initialized, will make the links passed in to it load their contents into the container specified. We've now duplicated the code we started out with. Granted, it's twice as many lines, but now we have something we can reuse and build upon. Let's dig into the new lines.

In the `initialize` method, we reference another method in the class:

```
this.attach();
```

The `this` keyword is very important. It references the instance of the class. So if on our page we create three instances, each instance can refer to itself as "this" and not run into the other instances. This is a really powerful concept, as it allows these little buckets of functionality to keep track of their own state. When you get the hang of using the `this` keyword, you'll see how it lets you make really clean code, even if you have a lot of `this` references all over the place, as evidenced in our `attach` method:

```
attach: function(){
```

This method, which is a property of every instance of our class, has no arguments. We could have specified some, but we don't need to since we stored our references to the links we want to monitor as `this.links`.

```
this.links.each(function(link){
```

We iterate over the links using the array method `each` as we did in our example in the previous chapter, but there's a difference here: `each` can take two arguments. In our previous example, we only used the first (a function to invoke with each item in the array), but not the second—an object to bind the `this` keyword to.

By default, the function you pass to an array in its iteration methods is bound to that array, so the `this` in the function references the array. But here we need `this` to reference our class so we can continue to reference it. So if we jump ahead to the end of this statement, we see

```
this.links.each(function(link){
    ...
}, this);
```

By specifying this second argument as a reference to our class, the function can reference `this` and point not to the array of links, but instead to our class. This is a little tricky, but it's very important (see "'this' and Binding" in the Appendix for more detail).

Inside our iteration, we add the event to the `link` just as we did in the previous chapter, but again, we have a subtle difference. Just like `Array.each`, `Element.addEvent` accepts as one of its arguments a function to invoke when the event is fired. If we want the contents of this inner function to be able to reference the `this` that refers to our class instance, we need to bind it to the function.

Unlike the array iteration methods, `addEvent` doesn't accept an additional argument for binding, so we must use the `bind` method on the `function` itself:

```
link.addEvent('click', function(event){
    ...
}.bind(this));
```

This is one of those gotcha things. `Array` and `Hash` iteration methods allow you to specify an argument for binding, but element event methods do not. Why doesn't MooTools make this consistent? Well, it's because the standards defined for JavaScript say otherwise, and where possible, MooTools follows those standards. Note that

```
myArray.each(function(){...}.bind(this))
```

will work, though it's not the "proper" way to do it. Moving on . . .

The last bit of code inside our `click` event looks very similar to the original example, with the only difference being that now we reference the container as `this.container`. It's because of this reference that we have to do the binding in the previous two lines. So, **if you don't reference `this` inside an inner function, you don't need to bind anything to it.**

```
link.addEvent('click', function(event){
  event.preventDefault();
  this.container.load(link.get('href'));
}.bind(this));
```

Instantiating Our Class

OK, so now we have a class that does what the previous example did. Now what? Just having a class doesn't do anything—you have to instantiate it. So our new page would look like this:

```
<!DOCTYPE html PUBLIC "-//W3C//DTD XHTML 1.0 Strict//EN"
  "http://www.w3.org/TR/xhtml1/DTD/xhtml1-strict.dtd">
<html xmlns="http://www.w3.org/1999/xhtml" xml:lang="en"
  lang="en" dir="ltr">
  <head>
    <meta http-equiv="Content-Type"
     content="text/html; charset=UTF-8" />
    <title>Your title</title>
    <script type="text/JavaScript"
     src="MooTools.js"></script>
    <script type="text/JavaScript">
      var AjaxTabs = new Class({
        initialize: function(container, links){
          this.container = $(container);
          this.links = $$(links);
          this.attach();
        },

        attach: function(){
          this.links.each(function(link){
            link.addEvent('click', function(event){
              event.preventDefault();
              this.container.load(link.get('href'));
            }.bind(this));
          }, this);
        }
      });
```

```
window.addEvent('domready', function(){
    new AjaxTabs($('pageContainer'),
                 $$('#pageLinks a'));
    });
</script>
</head>
<body>
    <ul id="pageLinks">
        <li><a href="/page1.html">page 1</a></li>
        <li><a href="/page2.html">page 2</a></li>
        <li><a href="/page3.html">page 3</a></li>
        <li><a href="/page4.html">page 4</a></li>
    </ul>
    <div id="pageContainer"></div>
</body>
</html>
```

Review

First, I'll again note that including all your JavaScript in the page like this isn't a best practice. You should include most of your code—especially reusable classes—in an external .js file. I'm putting it in the page here just to make the example easier to read.

We created a class that updates our page with the contents of the link URLs when clicked, and we can reuse that class in as many places as we want. As I outline in Chapter 1 in the section "Coding for Reuse," I prefer to think of the code I write in two ways: implementation code and reusable code. The preceding example highlights these two principals quite clearly: our class is designed to be reused and extended, and we could really use it anywhere we wanted to.

Classes, however, don't do anything unless you invoke them. Invoking a class is something you do with specific variables passed to them to configure them for a specific use, as with our example here where we create a new instance of our class with the links and container on the page. This code isn't reusable at all—it's quite specific to this page. When you build your site, your implementation code should be very light and as limited as much as possible to the things that are specific to a given page or a page's components, while the code that is shared across your site should be filled with classes that manage these components when they are initialized.

If you treat all the layout elements on your page this way, you'll end up with a much more manageable codebase as well as code you can reuse that you perhaps hadn't planned on reusing. It's actually quite common for me to write a class for a layout component thinking I'll never use it for anything else, only to find myself coming back to it to extend it for some other use. With that in mind, we'll make our class a little more flexible and extend it for greater reuse in the next chapter.

Chapter 15: Writing Flexible Classes

In the previous chapter, we wrote a class that featured a number of links that, when clicked, would update the contents of a container on the page. If we were to add a little bit of CSS styling, we might lay out the contents so it appears in a browser like this:

page 1   page 2   page 3   page 4

Page 1
Lorem ipsum dolor sit amet, consectetuer adipiscing elit. Aenean at nibh. Duis nec sem. In purus eros, adipiscing nec, ultricies ut, viverra nec, purus. Mauris ultrices, nisi nec tincidunt imperdiet, eros tortor fringilla lorem, eu eleifend justo sapien at massa. Quisque tincidunt leo in orci. Cum sociis natoque penatibus et magnis dis parturient montes, nascetur ridiculus mus. Donec at mauris eget ligula porttitor mollis. Nunc rutrum interdum lacus.

This pattern—tabs essentially—is one that's used a lot on web sites these days in lots of configurations. Look, here's Yahoo's home page:

If we wrote our `AjaxTabs` class a little more generically, maybe it would be more broadly useful. The question then is what things do we need to be able to configure for it to behave differently in different use cases?

Well, for starters, what if we didn't want to use Ajax to get the content? What if we wanted to let the user click a tab and just show the appropriate container of content that's already loaded on the page? Sure, if we need to fetch the information with Ajax, that should be an option, but if we already have the information, we shouldn't go get it again. So let's take the Ajax out of our little class, and then extend it so we can put the Ajax back in.

Also, while we're at it, let's add some options and events so we can configure our pages in ways that we might need to.

Step 1: Creating a Foundation Class

Starting with our example from the beginning of this chapter, let's re-create our tab class without the Ajax. Unlike the previous chapters, I'm not going to dissect the example line by line (as our code examples are going to start getting somewhat long). Instead, I'll include comments in the code briefly describing what each line is for.

A preface to this new version of the example: unlike the previous version, which used Ajax to update the contents of a single container, we're going to make this version hide and show the container that corresponds to the tab the user clicks. So if we have four tabs, we'll have four containers. If the user clicks the first tab, we'll show the first container and hide the others. Also, since we aren't fetching information via Ajax, we won't assume that the tabs are links, though they could be.

```
var Tabs = new Class({
  //We are going to store our tabs in an array that's
  //a property of the class - previously we called them
  //links, but they don't have to be anchor tags
  //anymore, so we'll be more generic with our name
  tabs: [],
  initialize: function(containers, tabs){
    //We need to make sure that the containers
    //and tabs are an Elements collection
    //so we pass them each through $$
    containers = $$(containers);
    //For each tab passed in, we'll iterate over it
    //and pass both the tab and the corresponding
    //container to our new method that adds sections for
    //us
    $$(tabs).each(function(tab, index){
      this.addSection(tab, containers[index]);
    }, this);
    this.show(0); //Show the first tab on startup
  },
```

```
    //Include the tab in the tabs array; use
    //.include in case for some reason, it's already
    //in there
    this.tabs.include(tab);
    //Store a reference between the tab and its
    //container
    tab.store('container', container);
    //Pass the tab to our attach method
    this.attach(tab);
  },
  //Our attach method has changed; now it takes
  //as its argument a single tab to monitor
  attach: function(tab){
    tab.addEvent('click', function(event){
      event.preventDefault();
      //And we send the instruction to display a
      //tab's content to a new "show" method, which
      //can be invoked at any time, not just here
      this.show(this.tabs.indexOf(tab));
    }.bind(this));
  },
  //Our show method takes the index of the item to show
  show: function(index){
    //At the end of this method we store the index that
    //is currently visible. If this method is called to
    //show the tab that's already visible, don't do
    //anything.
    if (this.current === index) return;
    //We iterate over each tab
    this.tabs.each(function(tab, i){
      //If the index we're showing matches the index of
      //the tab we're iterating over, then we set its
      //display style to block, otherwise we set it to
      //none to hide it
      var container = tab.retreive('container');
      if (index === i)
        container.setStyle('display', 'block');
      else container.setStyle('display', 'none');
```

```
    });
    this.current = index;
  }
});
```

And here's what it would look like to invoke this class:

```
<script>
window.addEvent('domready', function(){
  new Tabs($$('#tabContainers div.container'),
           $$('#tabs li'));
});
</script>
//The HTML for it would look something like this:
<ul id="tabs">
  <li>Tab 1</li>
  <li>Tab 2</li>
  <li>Tab 3</li>
</li>
<div id="tabContainers">
  <div class="container">This is the content
   for the first tab.</div>
  <div class="container">This is the content
   for the second tab.</div>
  <div class="container">This is the content
   for the third tab.</div>
  <div class="container">This is the content
   for the fourth tab.</div>
</div>
```

So this is our "foundation" class. It does all the basics of a tabbed interface, but there are three big things missing: options, events, and the ability to load the content via Ajax (which is where we started).

A Note on Using Methods

A quick thing to note that's new in this class from the previous chapter is the show method. Because we now have a method to show a specific tab, we could, in theory, change the tab at any time by referencing this method. For instance, let's say we had another link on the page somewhere and we wanted to change to the second tab if the user clicked it. We could do something like this:

```
var myTabs = new Tabs($$('div.container'),
                      $$('#tabs li'));
$('myOtherLink').addEvent('click', function(){
  myTabs.show(1); //Switch to the second tab
  return false; //Stop the event from propagating
});
```

This ability to reference the methods of the instance is obviously really useful. It allows you to create an instance of a class and then invoke the behaviors in that class when you need to. When you are authoring a class, consider how and where you'll want access to functionality like this and make these methods easy to use.

Step 2: Adding Options

Whenever you have a class that's designed to be used over and over again, it's almost always a good idea to identify the things in the class that you might want to tweak for a given implementation. Regarding the preceding code, here are some things we might want the class to allow us to do when we create instances of it:

- Add a CSS class to the selected tab and selected section.

- Specify a different "start" index (right now, the first tab is shown on startup).

There are potentially a lot of other things you might want to configure. You could make the sections fade in and out with effects. You could store a cookie with the state of the tabs so that it restores itself for users when they visit the page again. For our purposes, let's keep things simple and just add these two options: a CSS class for the selected tabs and sections, and the ability to specify a different start option.

Here's our class again, this time without all the earlier comments and with a few new lines I've emphasized in bold and commented about.

```
var Tabs = new Class({
  //Add the functionality of the Options class
  //to our class
  Implements: Options,
  options: {
    //The default value of our options
    //If we don't specify any of these, the
    //default values are used
    selectedTabCssClass: 'selected',
    selectedSectionCssClass: 'selected',
    firstShow: 0
  },
  tabs: [],
  //Our constructor now takes a 3rd argument: options
    initialize: function(containers, tabs, options){
    //Merge the options passed in by the user with those
    //defined by the class; note that it's OK if this
    //argument is undefined
    this.setOptions(options);
    containers = $$(containters);
    $$(tabs).each(function(tab, index){
      this.addSection(tab, containers[index]);
    }, this);
    //Show the panel specified in the options
    this.show(this.options.firstShow);
  },
  addSection: function(tab, container) {
    this.tabs.include(tab);
    tab.store('container', container);
    this.attach(tab);
  },
```

```
attach: function(tab) {
  tab.addEvent('click', function(event) {
    event.preventDefault();
    this.show(this.tabs.indexOf(tab));
  }.bind(this));
},
show: function(index) {
  if (this.current === index) return;
  this.tabs.each(function(tab, i) {
    var container = tab.retreive('container');
    //If we're showing the tab, add the CSS classes,
    //else remove them
    if (index === i) {
      tab.addClass(this.options.selectedTabCssClass);
      container.addClass(
        this.options.selectedSectionCssClass);
      container.setStyle('display', 'block');
    } else {
      tab.removeClass(
        this.options.selectedTabCssClass);
      container.removeClass(
        this.options.selectedSectionCssClass);
      container.setStyle('display', 'none');
    }
  }, this); //Now we're using 'this' inside this
            //funciton, so we must specify a binding
            //here to keep 'this' pointed to our
            //instance.
  this.current = index;
}
});
```

Adding options is pretty easy. You shouldn't go crazy with them, but in general, any place you can conceive of wanting to change a value for a specific instance is where you should add an option.

Let's look at how we'd invoke this class and specify different options.

```
window.addEvent('domready', function(){
  new Tabs($$('#tabContainers div.container'),
          $$('#tabs div.tab'), {
    selectedTabCssClass: "selectedTab",
    selectedSectionCSSClass: "selectedSection",
    firstShow: 2
  });
});
```

Note that you can specify only a portion of the options. Whichever options you don't specify will revert to the defaults specified in the class. So, if you invoked the class like this:

```
window.addEvent('domready', function(){
  new Tabs($$('#tabContainers div.container'),
          $$('#tabs div.tab'), {
    firstShow: 2
  });
});
```

then your instance would use "selected" for the selected tabs and sections CSS class, but the firstShow option would be changed from the default (zero) to what you specify here (two).

Step 3: Adding Events

Options let you configure your class to behave differently, while events let you attach additional functionality to your class. The best place to insert events are when the state changes in some way that you can't control or predict. For instance, an Ajax request sends off a request for data from the server, but you have no way of knowing how long that will take to get a response. If you want a function to be called when the data has returned, you need some hook into that event.

The same can be said when the unknown factor is the user. Consider dragging an element. If the user starts dragging an object, who can say when that user will stop? To handle the next step in the behavior—when the user drops what he or she has been dragging—we need a hook into that moment.

The Events class, not to be confused with the native Event class that extends the native browser event created when users click, mouseover, etc., allows us to add events to our classes so that these unpredictable moments have the hooks we need to manage the behavior we want.

Making Good Use of Events

Like options, we want to use events judiciously. There's no expense to having too many other than your code getting bloated, but at the same time we want to be able to quickly use our classes, so choosing the key points where an event is needed is important.

The other key to using events is passing the best arguments to the event when it is fired. Not only must you choose the best places to add events, but you also need to decide which values to pass, since when you fire an event, you can pass any number of values to it. This is important because you need to be able to do something with the event when you add hooks into the class. Let's reconsider the Ajax example we just discussed. Knowing that the server has returned something is only half the battle—we need to know *what* the server returned.

So with our tab layout class, what events occur that we might want to know about? Well, when the user clicks a tab, the tabs change. That might be useful information. What would we want to know when this occurs? Certainly, we'd want to know what tab is now currently visible. Maybe we'd also want to know which tab just got hidden? Given that we do these two things separately as we iterate over all the tabs, we can't have a single event, so instead we'll have to fire them each off separately—one for when a tab is shown, and another for when a tab is hidden.

Again, here's our class in its current form with the new code in bold:

```
var Tabs = new Class({
  //We're implementing two classes in now,
  //so we must use an array to specify both
  //items to be implemented
  Implements: [Options, Events],
  options: {
    selectedTabCssClass: 'selected',
    selectedSectionCssClass: 'selected',
    firstShow: 0,
    //Our class now has two events that you can specify
    //in the options
    onShow: $empty,
    onHide: $empty
  },
  tabs: [],
  initialize: function(containers, tabs, options){
    this.setOptions(options);
    containers = $$(containers);
    $$(tabs).each(function(tab, index){
      this.addSection(tab, containers[index]);
    }, this);
    this.show(this.options.firstShow);
  },
  addSection: function(tab, container) {
    this.tabs.include(tab);
    tab.store('container', container);
    this.attach(tab);
  },

  attach: function(tab){
    tab.addEvent('click', function(event){
      event.preventDefault();
      this.show(this.tabs.indexOf(tab));
    }.bind(this));
  },
```

```
  show: function(index){
    if (this.current === index) return;
    this.tabs.each(function(tab, i){
      var container = tab.retreive('container');
      if (index === i) {
        tab.addClass(this.options.selectedTabCssClass);
        container.addClass(
          this.options.selectedSectionCssClass);
        container.setStyle('display', 'block');
        //We must add the instruction to invoke, or
        //"fire," the event in our code where we think
        //is the most suitable time; here we fire it
        //after the container has been displayed
        this.fireEvent('onShow', [i, tab, container]);
      } else {
        tab.removeClass(
          this.options.selectedTabCssClass);
        container.removeClass(
          this.options.selectedSectionCssClass);
        container.setStyle('display', 'none');

        //If the current tab is the one we're iterating
        //on OR there is no currently visible tab
        //(because this is the first time we've called
        //this method), then fire the 'onHide' event
        if (this.current === i || !$chk(this.current))
          this.fireEvent('onHide', [i, tab, container]);
      }
    }, this);
    this.current = index;
  }
});
```

Now our class has events for both when a tab is displayed and when one is hidden. Note that in both cases we pass as arguments the index, the tab, and the container that have just been shown or hidden.

So let's look at what it's like to actually use these events. Let's say we want to show a tooltip when the user shows the fourth tab; maybe it has a form in it. The tooltip is out of context when the other tabs are displayed, so we need to show the tooltip when the fourth one is displayed, and hide it when the fourth one is hidden.

```javascript
window.addEvent('domready', function(){
  new Tabs($$('#tabContainers div.container'),
         $$('#tabs div.tab'), {
    //The function that's called when the event fires
    //is passed the index, the tab, and the container:
    onShow: function(index, tab, container){
      //If the fourth one is shown, show my tip
      if (index == 3)
        $('tip').setStyle('display', 'block');
    },
    //Hmmm. Here we're not using the tab and container
    //references. We can save a few keystrokes and just
    // not declare them; there's no harm if we do,
    //but we're not using them so we'll skip them:
    onHide: function(index) {
      //If the fourth one is hidden, hide my tip
      if (index == 3)
        $('tip').setStyle('display', 'none');
    }
  });
});
```

Adding Events After Invokation

In the preceding example, we create an instance of our tabs class and specify the `onHide` and `onShow` events in the options. This is some magic that's provided by the `Options` class. If it finds an option that begins with "on" and the value is a function, it'll treat it as an event. Note that when it encounters options like this, it removes them from the options object when it sets up the events.

But you can also use the `addEvent` method to attach your events after you've instantiated your class. This can be especially useful if you end up with more than one function that needs to be invoked when an event fires. The sytnax is the same for classes as it is for elements:

```
myTabs.addEvent('onShow', function(index, tab,
    container){ ..... });
```

You Don't Have to Declare Events in the Options Object

In our class, the options with events look like this:

```
var Tabs = new Class({
  Implements: [Options, Events],
  options: {
    selectedTabCssClass: 'selected',
    selectedSectionCssClass: 'selected',
    firstShow: 0,
    onShow: $empty,
    onHide: $empty
  },
  ...etc
```

In the options, we declare that the `onShow` and `onHide` events default to `$empty`, which is just an empty function. Because the `Options` method `setOptions` removes these values from the options object, you don't really have to declare them like this. There's no benefit. It doesn't hurt anything, but it doesn't get you anything.

Still, it's nice to be able to glance at the code and see what the options and events are, all right there at the top of the class. By convention, MooTools leaves these lines in the source code but comments them out. So if you look at any class in the MooTools library, you'll find these declarations present, but commented. This is a good practice (as it cuts down on your code size, even if only a little), and I follow it in my own code.

So, taking my own advice, our finished "foundation" class would look like this:

```
var Tabs = new Class({
  Implements: [Options, Events],
  options: {
    selectedTabCssClass: 'selected',
    selectedSectionCssClass: 'selected',
    firstShow: 0 //Don't forget to remove the trailing
                 //comma here as it's now the last
                 //item in this object
  /* onShow: $empty,
    onHide: $empty */
  },
  tabs: [],
  initialize: function(containers, tabs, options){
    this.setOptions(options);
    containers = $$(containers);
    $$(tabs).each(function(tab, index){
      this.addSection(tab, containers[index]);
    }, this);
    this.show(this.options.firstShow);
  },
  addSection: function(tab, container) {
    this.tabs.include(tab);
    tab.store('container', container);
    this.attach(tab);
  },
  attach: function(tab){
    tab.addEvent('click', function(event){
      event.preventDefault();
      this.show(this.tabs.indexOf(tab));
    }.bind(this));
  },
```

```
show: function(index){
  if (this.current === index) return;
  this.tabs.each(function(tab, i){
    var container = tab.retreive('container');
    if (index === i) {
      tab.addClass(this.options.selectedTabCssClass);
      container.addClass(
        this.options.selectedSectionCssClass);
      container.setStyle('display', 'block');
      this.fireEvent('onShow', [i, tab, container]);
    } else {
      tab.removeClass(
        this.options.selectedTabCssClass);
      container.removeClass(
        this.options.selectedSectionCssClass);
      container.setStyle('display', 'none');
      if (this.current === i || !$chk(this.current))
        this.fireEvent('onHide',
            [i, tab, container]);
    }
  }, this);
  this.current = index;
  }
});
```

Step 4: Extending the Class

Our Tabs class is looking pretty sweet. We can use it to create numerous instances on a page or across a site. Initializing it on any given page is only a line or two of code.

But wait a sec, we started this whole thing off with a tabbed area that loaded the content via Ajax. This new class doesn't do that. Let's extend our class to add Ajax back into the equation.

Identifying What Needs to Change

To get started altering our foundation class, we need to consider what we need to add or change. For starters, we're going to load the content in via Ajax, which means we need URLs for each tab. In our previous class (AjaxTabs in Chapter 14), each tab was a link. We got the URL from the link. That could work here, too, but maybe we want to make it optional to pass in a set of links instead. So we know we need some way to specify in the options what the links are.

What else? Well, maybe we want the option to cache the results. If the user clicks a tab, and we fetch the info for that tab from the server, there's no need to fetch it again if the user revisits the tab. These two changes will require new events and new options. First, let's add the options for the URLs and the caching.

```
var AjaxTabs = new Class({
  //Extend Tabs; unlike Implement, which lets
  //you implement any number of classes, Extends
  //can only take a single Class
  Extends: Tabs,
  options: {
    //By default, we'll cache the results
    cache: true,
    //This empty array is the default for the URLs
    //If the array remains empty, we'll try and get
    //the URL from the tab element and assume it has
    //an href property
    urls: []
  }
});
```

We now have a class that extends our Tabs class that has a few new options. Let's put those to use. Both of these options are going to be used when we load the information via Ajax. This means that our show method needs some additional logic.

```
var AjaxTabs = new Class({
  Extends: Tabs,
  options: {
    cache: true,
    urls: []
  },
  show: function(index, force){
    //Get the tab:
    var tab = this.tabs[index];
    //Get the URL from the options or, if that's not
    //set, see if the tab has an href property
    var url = this.options.urls[index] ||
             tab.get('href');
    //If the URL isn't set OR we're caching and the
    //tab's data is already loaded, OR we're forcing
    //this method then just show the new tab
    if (!url || force ||
        (this.options.cache && tab.retrieve('loaded'))) {
      //this.parent(index) executes the show method
      //in the Tabs class
      this.parent(index);
    } else {
      //Otherwise, we're going to fetch the data from
      //the server
      this.fetchTabContent(index, url);
    }
  },
```

```
fetchTabContent: function(index, url) {
    //Get the tab:
    var tab = this.tabs[index];
    //Get the container we're going to update:
    var container = tab.retrieve('container');
    //See if we've already got an instance
    //of Request.HTML for this tab:
    var request = tab.retrieve('tabAjax');
    //If not, we'll need to create one:
    if (!request) {
        request = new Request.HTML({
            //Tell it to insert the HTML into our container
            update: container,
            url: url, //Using the URL we got earlier
            onSuccess: function(){
                //Show the container, and force it not to
                //check for caching
                this.show(index, true);
                //On success the HTML is automatically
                //injected into our container, so all
                //that's left to do is set the loaded
                //flag:
                tab.store('loaded');
            }.bind(this) //Don't forget to bind the "this"
        });
        tab.store('tabAjax', request);
    }
    request.send();
}
});
```

Now our class will attempt to get the URL for each tab and then get the data from the server, update the container, and then show it. We reuse the instances of Request.HTML so that we don't create a race condition. We set a flag to cache the results if our options tell us to do so.

We now have two classes—Tabs, which handles the basic functionality of a tabbed layout, and AjaxTabs, which extends that class to add just the

Ajax bit. If, in the future, we decided to add more functionality to our `Tabs` class, our `AjaxTabs` class will automatically inherit that functionality.

Here's what it would look like to instantiate our extension:

```
var myAjaxTabs = new AjaxTabs($$('div.container'),
                              $$('div.tab'), {
  urls: ['/page1.html', '/page2.html',
         '/page3.html', '/page4.html']
});
//Or, if our tabs are links
var myAjaxTabs = new AjaxTabs($$('div.container'),
                             $$('a.tab'));
```

Adding a Few More Options and Events

```
var AjaxTabs = new Class({
  Extends: Tabs,
  options: {
    cache: true,
    urls: [],
    //Create the new option to be passed to Request
    requestOptions: {}
  },
  show: function(index, force){
    var tab = this.tabs[index];
    var url = this.options.urls[index] ||
              tab.get('href');
    if (!url || force ||
        (this.options.cache && tab.retrieve('loaded'))) {
      this.parent(index);
    } else {
    this.fetchTabContent(index, url);
    }
  },
  fetchTabContent: function(index, url) {
    var tab = this.tabs[index];
    var container = tab.retrieve('container');
    var request = tab.retrieve('tabAjax');
```

```
      if (!request) {
        //Here things get tricky; we need to merge the
        //options with the data for this tab; we put the
        //tab data last to make sure it overwrites
        //anything in the options
        request = new Request.HTML(
          $merge(this.options.requestOptions, {
            update: container,
            url: url,
            //Additionally, we need to allow for
            //the options to specify their own
            //onSuccess method, so we'll remove
            //ours from the options and add our
            //event to the instance
            onSuccess: function(){
              tab.store('loaded', true);
              this.parent(index);
            }.bind(this)
          })
        //Here we attach our own onSuccess method. If
        //there's an onSuccess method in the options,
        //it'll fire before ours
        ).addEvent('onSuccess', function(){
          tab.store('loaded', true);
          this.show(index, true)
        }.bind(this));
        tab.store('tabAjax', request);
      }
      request.send();
    }
  });
```

This was a little tricky. We create an empty object in our options for the
options to be passed along to the Request.HTML instance, but we need to
specify the URL and the DOM element to update based on which tab got
clicked. We use $merge to combine the two, making sure our URL and
container are preserved by making them the second argument sent to

`$merge`. Additionally, since the options might include an `onSuccess` method, we need to move our method out of the options so they don't collide. We do this by using the `addEvent` method to attach our event after we create the instance. So long as we add this event before we send the request, we won't have a problem. You can have as many functions attached to an event as you like.

Here's what that might look like in use:

```
var myAjaxTabs = new AjaxTabs($$('div.container'),
$$('div.tab'), {
  urls: ['/page1.html', '/page2.html',
         '/page3.html', '/page4.html'],
  requestOptions: {
    //Stop requests if the user clicks another tab
    //before the previous one loads:
    link: 'cancel',
    evalScripts: true,
    onSuccess: function(response){
      alert('Hey, ajax worked! Here\'s the response: '
         + response);
    }
  }
});
```

Review

We've now written two classes. The first one lets us manage tabs, and the second one adds Ajax functionality. Now we can initialize our classes on our pages with only a line or two of code. We can configure the behavior and manage several different types of uses, all with the same code. Nice!

Here's the code in its entirety without all the messy comments:

```
var Tabs = new Class({
  Implements: [Options, Events],
  options: {
    selectedTabCssClass: 'selected',
    selectedSectionCssClass: 'selected',
    firstShow: 0
/*  onShow: $empty,
    onHide: $empty */
  },
  tabs: [],
  initialize: function(containers, tabs, options){
    this.setOptions(options);
    $$(tabs).each(function(tab, index){
      this.addSection(tab, $$(containers)[index]);
    }, this);
    this.show(this.options.firstShow);
  },
  addSection: function(tab, container) {
    this.tabs.include(tab);
    tab.store('container', container);
    this.attach(tab);
  },
  attach: function(tab){
    tab.addEvent('click', function(event){
      event.preventDefault();
      this.show(this.tabs.indexOf(tab));
    }.bind(this));
  },
```

```
    show: function(index){
      if (this.current === index) return;
      this.tabs.each(function(tab, i){
        var container = tab.retreive('container');
        if (index === i) {
          tab.addClass(this.options.selectedTabCssClass);
          container.addClass(
            this.options.selectedSectionCssClass);
          container.setStyle('display', 'block');
          this.fireEvent('onShow', [i, tab, container]);
        } else {
          tab.removeClass(
            this.options.selectedTabCssClass);
          container.removeClass(
            this.options.selectedSectionCssClass);
          container.setStyle('display', 'none');
          if (this.current === i || !$chk(this.current))
            this.fireEvent('onHide',
              [i, tab, container]);
        }
      }, this);
      this.current = index;
    }
});

var AjaxTabs = new Class({
  Extends: Tabs,
  options: {
    cache: true,
    urls: [],
    requestOptions: {}
  },
```

```
show: function(index, force){
  var tab = this.tabs[index];
  var url = this.options.urls[index] ||
            tab.get('href');
  if (!url || force ||
      (this.options.cache && tab.retrieve('loaded'))) {
    this.parent(index);
  } else {
    this.fetchTabContent(index, url);
  }
},
fetchTabContent: function(index, url) {
  var tab = this.tabs[index];
  var container = tab.retrieve('container');
  var request = tab.retrieve('tabAjax');
  if (!request) {
    request = new Request.HTML(
      $merge(this.options.requestOptions, {
        update: container,
        url: url
      })
    ).addEvent('onSuccess', function(){
      tab.store('loaded', true);
      this.show(index, true)
    }.bind(this));
    tab.store('tabAjax', request);
  }
  request.send();
}
});
```

Chapter 16: Where to Learn More

Once you have the hang of writing JavaScript with MooTools, and this book doesn't seem to have any more secrets for you to uncover, there's still a lot of resources you can turn to for improving your skills.

The first place to start is MooTools itself. Look inside the code and try and pick apart some of its classes. The effects series of classes start with a very abstract foundation class (`Fx`), which is extended to add layers that are easier to worry with (`Fx.Tween`, `Fx.Morph`). Studying things like this will not only help you understand MooTools more, but also see new ways of doing things.

Write some classes of your own. Post them to the forums at MooTools.net (`http://forum.mootools.net`) and seek feedback. If you really want to get feedback, write a plug-in and release it. All of the classes I've released on CNET's Clientside result in a lot of feedback from people trying to use them.

I also recommend the following blogs, which often discuss JavaScript (some of them cover nothing else):

- **The MooTools Blog**: `http://blog.mootools.net`

- **Ajaxian**: `http://www.ajaxian.com`

- **Clientside**: `http://clientside.cnet.com`

- **Dean Edward's Blog**: `http://dean.edwards.name/weblog/`

- **Solutoire**: `http://www.solutoire.com`

- **d'bug**: `http://blog.reindel.com/`

- **Snook**: `http://www.snook.ca`

- **Alternate Idea**: `http://www.alternateidea.com`

There's one last resource on MooTools that often escapes the notice of many people, and that's probably because it's not well publicized. MooTools has an IRC channel:

```
irc://irc.freenode.net/mootools
```

You'll often find the principal developer (Valerio Proietti) hanging out there, along with several members of the development team.

Appendix: Core Concepts in JavaScript

There are a handful of important concepts that you need to be aware of with JavaScript, and if you aren't aware of them, stuff just won't work.

DOCTYPE Matters

It's important that you use a proper document type. I recommend XHTML Strict, but others will work (XHTML Transitional, for example). Here's an example of a strict DOCTYPE:

```
<!DOCTYPE html PUBLIC "-//W3C//DTD XHTML 1.0 Strict//EN"
   "http://www.w3.org/TR/xhtml1/DTD/xhtml1-strict.dtd">
<html xmlns="http://www.w3.org/1999/xhtml" xml:lang="en"
   lang="en" dir="ltr">
   <head>
```

There's sample documentation online about document types and how they work. I don't spend much time thinking about the subject and just use Strict all the time.

If you don't specify a DOCTYPE or if you use one that isn't XHTML, you'll get strange results when you try and use several of the classes and effects in MooTools.

Type Coercion: "Falsy" and "Truthy" Values

JavaScript's conditionals will do type coercion, and this is an important thing to know about, because if you don't, you can get into trouble. It's not a bad thing (if you ask me), so long as you know what to watch out for. In fact, it's quite useful for writing concise code.

What do I mean by type coercion? Consider this example:

```
var x = 0;
if (x) alert('x is truthy!');
```

In the preceding code, the alert will never execute because JavaScript interprets zeros as being "falsy." The same is true for empty strings, `undefined`, `null`, `NaN` (Not a Number), and, of course, `false`.

Further, try this code out in your browser (in the Firebug console for example):

```
0 == "" //true!
false == 0 //true!
false == "" //true!
```

Note that this really only applies to items that are coerced. For example:

```
"3" == 3
"false" != false //Though "false" == true,
                 //and for that matter, so does "true"
```

Also note that if you are referring to objects in memory (arrays, objects, i.e., {}, etc.) can be coerced as true, but never anything else. You don't have to work about `"3,2,1" == [3,2,1]` or anything.

Further, if you do the following:

```
{} == {}
[] == []
[1,2,3] == [1,2,3]
```

they are all false, because they are not the same object, despite the fact that they are both arrays or objects with equal values.

You can force type coercion by using the `!` and `!!` to produce Booleans:

```
var x = !!"foo"; //x is true
var x = !"foo"; //x is false
```

To avoid type coercion, you must use `===` and `!==` if you wish to be explicit:

```
var x = 0;
if (!x) alert ('x is falsy!');
if (x !== false) alert('x is NOT *false*');
```

Type coercion is not always a bad thing. In fact, it's used throughout MooTools, and there are even some methods that help you work with it more explicitly. Here's an example of how type coercion might be used:

```
var anchors = document.getElementsByTagName('a');
if (anchors.length) setup(anchors);
```

Here we save a few keystrokes (instead of writing `if (anchors.length > 0)`), but sometimes what you need to evaluate could be `null`, `undefined`, or an empty string, and writing a conditional to deal with all of those possibilities is more than two or three keystrokes.

Functional Programming (a.k.a. Lambda)

JavaScript is one of the most popular functional programming languages, but it's not alone. To quote from the Wikipedia page on the subject:

Pure functional programming languages typically enforce referential transparency, which is the notion that "equals can be substituted for equals": if two expressions have "equal" values (for some notion of equality), then one can be substituted for the other in any larger expression without affecting the result of the computation.

```
http://en.wikipedia.org/wiki/Functional_programming
```

Functional programming can be illustrated with the following examples:

```
function sum(x,y) {
   return x+y;
}
//Passing the result of the sum function as an argument
alert(sum(1,2));
//Has the same result as storing that value in
//a variable:
var onePlusTwo = sum(1,2);
alert(onePlusTwo);
//But the same thing could be accomplished with
//an anonymous function:
alert(function(x,y){ return x+y; }(1,2));
```

Here you can see how the result of all three alerts will be the same. The first and third examples evaluate a function as an argument to another one, passing the result as the argument.

This is also how a practice called *chaining* works. A function returns a value that contains its own methods, which can be executed immediately:

```
['one','two','three'].concat(['four']).toString();
```

First, we have an array with three values, and we execute a method called `concat`, which returns the array. When we execute `toString`, we are executing it on the result returned from `concat`.

It's very common practice to use these patterns in MooTools and JavaScript in general, and understanding them will make it easier to understand the examples in this book and the code you see in MooTools and elsewhere.

Literals and Anonymous Functions

Two very common patterns that you'll see in MooTools and other JavaScript frameworks are the use of literal declarations and anonymous functions.

Literal declarations are an alternative to declaring a value into a variable namespace. This is often done when passing arguments to a function. If a function accepts an array or an object, you can pass it one without declaring it first:

```
function sumArrayValues(array){
  var value = 0;
  for (var i = 0; i < array.length; i++){
    value += array[i];
  }
  return value;
};
var sum = sumArrayValues([0,1,1,3,5,8]); //sum is 18
```

Here we've passed an array (`[0,1,1,3,5,8]`) to our function without
defining that array into a variable namespace. This pattern is often used for
numbers, strings, functions, arrays, and objects:

```
//An object literal:
armNinjas({
   swords: 10,
   stars: 99,
   flyingGuillotines: 1
});
//An anonymous function:
setNinjaAttackMethod(function(weapons){
   ninja.leftHand = weapons.sword;
   ninja.righHand = weapons.star;
});
//Strings and numbers are much more familiar
//10 here a literal number; it isn't defined into
//a variable. Same goes for "poisoned":
giveNinjaStars(10, "poisoned");
```

"this" and Binding

JavaScript has a somewhat irregular scope schema that takes a little getting
used to. For starters, the *only* things that have scope are functions.
Conditional statements and iterations (`if`/`else`, `try`/`catch`, and `for`
loops, `while`, `switch`, etc.) don't have scope; only functions do.

The other concept, which is a little hard to grok, is the `this` keyword. `this`
is a pointer to an object that represents the current scope. By default, `this`
is the `window` DOM object. When you declare a variable name or a
function in your code, you are creating a property of the `window`. Thus,
these are all the same thing:

```
var x = 10;
alert(window.x); //10
alert(x); //10
alert(this.x); //10
```

Inside of a function you have a scope, but things can escape out of it. For example:

```
function test(){
    x = 10;
    var y = 20;
};
test();
alert(window.x);  //10
alert(window.y);  //undefined
```

By declaring the variable y using the var prefix, we confine that variable to the test function's scope. When you declare a variable without the var prefix, the JavaScript parser will attempt to find a reference to that variable in the current scope, and, if it cannot find it, it will search the parent scope and the parent's parent until it reaches and searches the window scope. If it finds the variable, it will change it; otherwise it will create that variable in the global namespace (the window). This was intended to make JavaScript easier for people who weren't used to writing code; however, if you ask me, it is just another example of the authors of the language trying to make it more forgiving but instead making it more unclear, but I digress.

OK, so now you understand how functions have scope. The next thing that you need to understand is that, in JavaScript, *everything* inherits from the Object prototype (see "Prototypal Inheritance" later in this appendix). The Object prototype has a few methods, none of which are very useful (see http://developer.mozilla.org/en/docs/Core_JavaScript_1.5_R eference:Global_Objects:Object).

So functions extend this prototype and add their own methods. Array does the same, and so does String, Number, Element, and so on.

Because functions are objects, you can assign properties to them. For example:

```
function foo(){};
foo.message = 'bar';
foo.say = function(){alert(foo.message)};
```

Here's where the this keyword comes into play. JavaScript allows you to invoke a function or method (a method is just a function that is a property of an object) by calling it (foo()) or by using the new constructor (new foo()). When you put new in front of the function call, the function is executed, and the object that represents that object invocation is returned. As I stated, this concept is a little tough to wrap your head around, but it's very important. Here's an illustration:

```
function Ninja(side, weapons) {
   this.side = side;
   this.weapons = weapons;
};
var goodNinja = new Ninja('good', ['sword','star',
   'Five-Point Palm Exploding Heart Technique']);
//goodNinja.side == 'good'
```

If you had just executed Ninja with those values, it would assign them to this which, in the *default* scope, is the window object. By using the new constructor, the Ninja function is executed, and the this of that invocation (Ninja) is returned.

Note   Because there is no distinction in the language between functions that are meant to be invoked with and without the new constructor, by convention capital letters are used for functions that are meant to use the constructor.

Binding

As outlined previously, the this keyword represents an object that is the current scope. By default it is the window object, but when you use a constructor (with the new prefix), you get back an object that represents the scope inside that function.

```
function whatsThis(){
   alert(this);
};
whatsThis(); //Window
new whatsThis(); //Object - the object for
                 //this invocation of whatsThis
```

When you just call a function, the this is the scope from which you call it. What this means is that it's possible to instruct a function what the this scope should be. By default, yes, it's the window, but you can also tell a function to use a different this. But why would you?

Turns out, there are a LOT of reasons. You'll use this ability *all the time*. Sometimes it's kind of crazy how much you'll want to use it, which is why it's crucial that you understand it well before you start really using MooTools.

Because MooTools makes use of the functional programming concepts outlined in previously in this appendix, you'll pass functions as arguments to other functions. Let's take the Array.each extension that MooTools adds to the Array prototype. Array.each takes two arguments: a function and an object to be used for binding (the latter is optional). Here's an example of it in action:

```
['blue','green','yellow'].each(function(value, index){
   alert('item ' + index + ' is ' + value);
   //Alerts:
   // "item 0 is 'blue'"
   // "item 1 is 'green'"
   // "item 2 is 'yellow'"
   if (index == this.length-1) this[index] = 'orange';
   //Changes the last item in the array to 'orange'
});
```

In this example, we pass an anonymous function to the `each` method. The `each` method loops through the items in the array and invokes the function. Because the method invoking that function is a property of the array, the `this` keyword points to the array. Our function can reference the array only by using the `this` keyword (how else could it?).

Consider this example:

```
var example = {
  say: function(msg) {alert(msg); },
  count: function(){
    [1,2,3].each(function(number) {
      this.say(number);
    });
  }
};
```

Now wait a second. Here we're trying to reference the `say` method, and we could because inside the `count` method the `this` keyword points to the `example` object. But we've already seen that the function that we pass to `Array.each` has its `this` keyword mapped to the array. We need to instruct this function that its `this` is NOT the array—it's the `example` object.

And that's what binding does. It lets us tell a function what its `this` is:

```
var example = {
  say: function(msg) { alert(msg); },
  count: function(){
    [1,2,3].each(function(number) {
      this.say(number);
    }, this); //Here's the important part!
  }
};
```

By passing along the `this` context here, we now can reference `example.say` inside our `each` function.

I said earlier that `this` gets used a LOT in MooTools, and it does. It's a core concept of JavaScript, so it's not just MooTools that makes use of it. There are countless examples of where it's used, but principally it's used where functions are passed as arguments. Other cases exist, but typically you'll apply it to anonymous functions.

Some methods (like `each`) allow you to pass the bound object as an argument, but not always. When this isn't an option, you'll have to use the `bind` method that's added to the native `function` object by MooTools. Here's an example of that in action:

```
//Imagine this code is inside of a broader scope, as
//with the previous example
$('myElement').addEvent('click', function(){
  this.say('clicked!');
}.bind(this)); //Here's the important bit
```

When you start digging into Chapters 13 and on where we start actually looking at MooTools in action, you'll see lots of references to binding, and you'll start to get an idea of all the places where this practice comes into play. Simply put, binding and the `this` keyword are two of the most important concepts to grasp in modern JavaScript-ing.

Closures

One concept in JavaScript that is quite powerful is *closure*. A closure is a function declared or evaluated in a scope with bound variables, i.e., variables declared in the same scope as a function are accessible by that function. Another way to put this is that the scope of an inner function continues to exist even after the parent function has returned.

Let's consider this function, which will change the color of a box from white to black:

```
function fadeToBlack(element){
  var now = 16;
  var fade = function(){
    var hex = level.toString(16);
    element.style.backgroundColor =
      "#"+hex+hex+hex+hex+hex+hex;
    if (now > 0) {
      now++;
      setTimeout(fade, 50);
    }
  }
  setTimeout(fade, 50);
};
```

When `fadeToBlack` is executed, it will evaluate the two variable declarations (`now` and `fade`), and then the `setTimeout` instruction, and then exit. 50 milliseconds later, the inner method `fade` will be executed, and it in turn references the inner variable `now`. This illustrates what a closure is in that both `fade` and `now` still exist in memory even though their parent function (`fadeToBlack`) has completed. Indeed, `fade` will be called 16 times over the course of a second and a half, and each time it will reference `now`, which was declared outside `fade`'s scope.

This is a very powerful and expressive convention in functional languages.

Prototypal Inheritance

JavaScript's inheritance model is somewhat different from many other languages that sport a classical inheritance model. In JavaScript, objects that inherit from other objects have a hidden link to their parent. This hidden link is a property called `prototype`. So, for example, all arrays inherit from the `Array` prototype, and you can reference that prototype by referencing `Array.prototype`. Using this reference, you can alter the prototype and therefore alter all arrays. If you wanted to add a method to

Array called sum that would add up all the values in an array that were numbers, you could:

```
Array.prototype.sum = function(){
   var result = 0;
   for (var i = 0; i < this.length; i++) {
   var value = parseInt(this[i]);
   if (!isNaN(value)) result += value;
   }
   return result;
}
alert([1,2,3].sum()); //Alerts "6"
```

All objects in JavaScript begin with the native Object prototype. Functions, Arrays, Numbers, Strings, and so forth all inherit from Object, which is one of the reasons why altering the Object prototype is considered forbidden.

What this means is that, say, Functions can have properties just like Objects can. So can Arrays. In the example, Array.sum is just a property of the Array prototype. You could also define that method for a specific array rather than all of them. For example:

```
var numbers = [1,2,3];
numbers.sum = function(){
   var result = 0;
   for (var i = 0; i < this.length; i++) {
   var value = parseInt(this[i]);
   if (!isNaN(value)) result += value;
   }
   return result;
}
alert(numbers.sum()); //Alerts "6"
```

The result here is that we've added a property to the array that isn't a value of the array's contents (1, 2, 3). Similarly, we can define properties of a function:

```
var ninja = function(){};
ninja.hiding = false;
ninja.hide = function(){ ninja.hiding = true};
```

Here we have a function (that doesn't do anything) called `ninja`. We define properties of that function just as if it were an object. Using binding, functions can reference themselves with the `this` keyword:

```
ninja.hide = function(){
   this.hiding = true
}.bind(ninja);
```

The Inheritance Chain

With prototypal inheritance, objects are first inspected for properties of their own, and, if an object does not have a property, then the object's prototype is inspected, and, if not found there, then *that* object's prototype is inspected, and on up the chain. So, if, for example, we had an inheritance chain like this:

```
Animal > Human > Ninja
```

and we referenced properties of `Ninja`, first the `Ninja` object would be inspected for that property to get the value, and if it wasn't found, then `Human` would be inspected, and then `Animal`.

Let's say that we had the following:

```
Animal = function(){};
Animal.isAlive = true;
//Human inherits from Animal
Human.hasOpposableThumbs = true;
//Ninja inherits from Human
Ninja.throwStar = function(target){
   target.isAlive = false
};
var redNinja = new Ninja();
```

Don't worry about *how* the inheritance gets applied, that's what MooTools helps you do (see the discussion on classes in Chapter 7).

If our code references `redNinja.isAlive`, the `Ninja` object doesn't have that property, so `Human` is inspected. `Human` doesn't have that property either, so it goes up the chain to `Animal`, which does have that property.

This is not to say that all instances of `Human` or `Ninja` share the same value for that property. It's more like saying that the default value for all `Humans` and `Ninjas` is that their property `isAlive` is true.

If we were to execute the code:

```
redNinja.isAlive = false;
```

in addition to being sad because our ninja has died, what we would observe is that now `redNinja` has its own property for `isAlive`. The `Animal` prototype still has an `isAlive` property with the value of `true`, but when we inspect `redNinja.isAlive`, we don't go up the chain to the prototype because `redNinja` has that property.

One of the little gotchas that can occur here is that it is possible to delete a property from an object. If that property is defined for an object's prototype, deleting the value from the object does not necessarily mean that the value is now `undefined`.

Consider this:

```
//Continuing from the preceding code
//where the chain is Animal > Human > Ninja
//and Animal.isAlive defaults to true
redNinja.isAlive = false;
if(!redNinja.isAlive)
   alert("Oh what grief, our ninja is dead!");
delete redNinja.isAlive;
if(redNinja.isAlive) alert("Oh happy day! Our ninja is
alive again!");
```

By deleting the `isAlive` property from our `Ninja` instance, we revert back to the value contained in `Animal`.

This inheritance model—the prototypal inheritance model—is different from Classical inheritance and can take some getting used to. Thankfully, MooTools has tools to help us manage these relationships.

Unobtrusive JavaScripting

It's good practice to have as little JavaScript in your actual document as possible. Opinions differ on whether JavaScript is best served externally or as a long string at the top of the document (for speed purposes), but it's now common practice to avoid having JavaScript mixed in with your HTML.

Even if you decide for your own design purposes to deliver JavaScript with the page (and sometimes it makes sense to do this), you should separate the JavaScript from the HTML. Not only does this make it easier to manage your code base, but it also makes your layouts more reusable.

So, for example, compare the following two examples:

"Intrusive" JavaScript:

```
<a href="http://foo.com"
 onclick="someFunction()">click me!</a>
```

"Unobtrusive" JavaScript:

```
<a href="http://foo.com" id="clickMe">click me!</a>
<script>
//This is MooTools syntax
$('clickMe').addEvent('click', someFunction);
</script>
```

While both examples work just fine, the latter example is much easier to find and understand. When you pepper your HTML with function calls, it's difficult to maintain, especially when things get complicated (and when you're using Ajax to replace content and effects to fade stuff in and out, it gets even more complicated!). Additionally, if you deliver your JavaScript externally, your HTML documents will be clean, vanilla HTML and are more likely to degrade gracefully when things go wrong.

Additionally, by using unobtrusive methods, you can add more than one event to an element, or remove an event at a later time.

Note   The JavaScript compiler in the browser has an odd feature: when the compiler encounters an error, it attempts to replace the nearby end of line with a semicolon and parse again. This was designed to make JavaScript "easier" for an audience that may not be used to strict standards in the things they were normally writing (in theory, HTML). The result is that if you have code that does not have a semicolon at the end of every declaration, the compiler will insert them for you. However, when compressing JavaScript, all line breaks are removed, which means that if you have any lines that are lacking semicolons, your code will break. *Always put semicolons at the end of any of your declarations.* Example:

```
var ninja;
var ninja.visible = false;
var assassinate = function(ninja, target){
  ninja.kill(target);
};
ninja.weapons = ['star','sword','surprise'];
//You do NOT have to put semicolons at the
//end of statements no semicolon necessary after
//if/else, for, while, etc.
if (target.isAlive){ ninja.kill(target);}
for(var i = 0; i < targets.length; i++){
  ninja.kill(target[i]);
}
```

DomReady

Unobtrusive JavaScripting has a downside, though. In order to add functionality to the document (more specifically the Document Object Model, or DOM), you have to wait for the DOM to load. You can only collect elements from the DOM if they are in memory, which means your code can't safely run until the document is loaded.

Traditionally, the `window.onload` event was used for executing such code, but the `onload` event fires only after all the HTML has loaded *and* all the assets in it (the images, CSS, JavaScript, etc.). By the time every image and advertisement has loaded, the user can see the page and in some cases has already clicked something on the page, and it's too late to execute your code.

This is where the `DomReady` event comes into play. This event is added to the DOM by MooTools and fires as soon as the HTML is in memory but doesn't wait for any assets to load. By attaching your DOM scripting code to `DomReady`, you can usually execute your code before the layout is drawn by the browser.

```
<script>
//Execute my method attack when the DOM is loaded
window.addEvent('domready', ninjas.attack);
</script>
```

You can find more information on how `addEvent` and `DomReady` work in Chapters 5 and 6, respectively.

Namespacing

When writing implementation code—code that isn't meant to be reused, but instead sets up all the actions and functionality for a page (for example, turn these images into a slide show, expose this content when the user clicks that link, etc.)—a common practice is to make all the variables and functions members of an object.

This practice pays several dividends. Most notably, you don't have to worry about another bit of code overwriting your function and variable names. So long as the namespace you choose is unique, any property you add to it is safe. Additionally, it helps keep your code organized and tidy.

```
<script>
var ninjas = {
  function: attack(){
    for(var i = 0; i < ninjas.targets.length; i++){
      ninjas.kill(ninjas.targets[i]);
    }
  },
  kill: function(target){
    target.isAlive = false;
  },
  targets: ['fred', 'bill', 'white ninja']
};
ninjas.attack(); //!!!
</script>
```

By assigning functions and variables as members of a single namespace, it doesn't matter the order that they are declared; you can reference members that are not yet defined, and you don't have to worry about someone using the function name `kill` because yours is in the `ninjas` namespace.

Related Titles

Snook, Jonathan et al. *Accelerated DOM Scripting with Ajax, APIs, and Libraries*. Berkeley, CA: Apress, 2007

Copyright

MooTools Essentials: The Official MooTools Reference for JavaScript™ and Ajax Development

© 2008 by Aaron Newton

ISBN-13 (electronic): 978-1-4302-0984-3

ISBN-13 (paperback): 978-1-4302-0983-6

Trademarked names may appear in this book. Rather than use a trademark symbol with every occurrence of a trademarked name, we use the names only in an editorial fashion and to the benefit of the trademark owner, with no intention of infringement of the trademark.

Java™ and all Java-based marks are trademarks or registered trademarks of Sun Microsystems, Inc., in the United States and other countries. Apress, Inc., is not affiliated with Sun Microsystems, Inc., and this book was written without endorsement from Sun Microsystems, Inc.

Distributed to the book trade in the United States by Springer-Verlag New York, Inc., 233 Spring Street, 6th Floor, New York, NY 10013, and outside the United States by Springer-Verlag GmbH & Co. KG, Tiergartenstr. 17, 69112 Heidelberg, Germany.

In the United States: phone 1-800-SPRINGER, fax 201-348-4505, e-mail orders@springer-ny.com, or visit http://www.springer-ny.com. Outside the United States: fax +49 6221 345229, e-mail orders@springer.de, or visit http://www.springer.de.

For information on translations, please contact Apress directly at 2855 Telegraph Ave, Suite 600, Berkeley, CA 94705. Phone 510-549-5930, fax 510-549-5939, e-mail info@apress.com, or visit http://www.apress.com.

Printed in the United States
204349BV00009B/27-34/P

9 781430 209836